Mahatma Gandhi

Titles in the series Critical Lives present the work of leading cultural figures of the modern period. Each book explores the life of the artist, writer, philosopher or architect in question and relates it to their major works.

Mahatma Gandhi

Douglas Allen

REAKTION BOOKS

Published by Reaktion Books Ltd
33 Great Sutton Street
London EC1V ODX, UK

www.reaktionbooks.co.uk

First published 2011

Printed and bound in Great Britain
by Bell & Bain, Glasgow

British Library Cataloguing in Publication Data
Allen, Douglas, 1941–
    Mahatma Gandhi. – (Critical lives)
    1. Gandhi, Mahatma, 1869–1948.
    2. Gandhi, Mahatma, 1869–1948 – Philosophy.
    3. Gandhi, Mahatma, 1869–1948 – Influence.
    4. Statesman – India – Biography.
    I. Title II. Series
    947'.0841'092-DC22

ISBN 978 1 86189 865 4

Contents

In the midst of death life persists, in the midst of untruth truth persists, in the midst of darkness light persists.

M.K. Gandhi
Young India, 11 October 1928

Gandhi's faith in *Sayta* (truth).

Introduction

Mohandas Karamchand Gandhi was and continues to be arguably the most admired human being of the twentieth century in India and throughout the world. Polls invariably rank Gandhi at or near the top of the most admired, along with Albert Einstein and a few others. M. K. Gandhi is better known as *Mahatma* ('Great Soul') Gandhi, the honorific title usually believed to have been conferred upon him and certainly popularized by Nobel Laureate Rabindranath Tagore.[1] In India he was frequently given the honorific title *Bapu* ('Father'), and he is honoured in India as the Father of the Nation. His birthday, 2 October, is celebrated in India as *Gandhi Jayanti*, a national holiday. After the United Nations General Assembly vote of 15 June 2007, his birthday is celebrated worldwide as the 'International Day of Non-Violence'.

Remarkably, Mahatma Gandhi was and continues to be admired by a range and diversity of people. Such admiration was expressed by millions of illiterate peasants, who identified with and often worshipped and even deified him. Of the Indian leaders in the Freedom Movement, he alone was able to capture the imagination, love and trust of the impoverished peasants and to inspire them to transform their values and commitments. As Tagore observed: 'Mahatma Gandhi came and stood at the door of India's destitute millions, clad as one of themselves, speaking to them in their own language . . . who else has so unreservedly accepted the vast masses of the Indian people as his flesh and blood . . . Truth Awakened Truth.'

Such admiration was also expressed by many of the best-known cultural, political and scientific figures of Gandhi's lifetime. In what is probably the most frequently cited tribute to Gandhi, made on the occasion of Gandhi's seventieth birthday, Albert Einstein declared: 'Generations to come, it may be, will scarcely believe that such a one as this ever in flesh and blood walked upon this earth.' On another occasion Einstein wrote: 'I believe that Gandhi's views were the most enlightened of all the political men in our time. We should strive to do things in his spirit: not to use violence in fighting for our cause, but by non-participation in anything you believe is evil.'

On 30 January 1948 Pandit Jawaharlal Nehru, India's first prime minister, broadcast to the nation that 'the light has gone out of our lives and there is darkness everywhere . . . Our beloved leader, Bapu as we called him, the Father of the Nation, is no more.'[2] Nehru continues that he was wrong in stating that the light has gone out. Even a thousand years later, he said, the light that had illuminated India 'will still be seen in this country and the world will see it and it will give solace to innumerable hearts. For that light represented something more than the immediate present; it represented the living, the eternal truths, reminding us of the right path, drawing us from error, taking this ancient country to freedom.'

Civil rights leader Martin Luther King Jr often spoke of his admiration for and indebtedness to Gandhi in his theory and practice of nonviolence and nonviolent activism. In the section 'Pilgrimage to Nonviolence' in his book *Stride Toward Freedom*, King writes: 'Gandhi was probably the first person in history to lift the love ethic of Jesus above mere interaction between individuals to a powerful and effective social force on a large scale.' King says that the intellectual and moral satisfaction that he failed to gain from

Pandit Jawaharlal Nehru sharing a joke with Gandhi, Mumbai, 6 July 1946.

Bentham and Mill, Marx and Lenin, Hobbes, Rousseau and Nietzsche, he 'found in the non-violent resistance philosophy of Gandhi'. According to King, 'If humanity is to progress, Gandhi is inescapable. He lived, thought, and acted, inspired by the vision of humanity evolving toward a world of peace and harmony. We may ignore him at our own risk.'

At the same time Gandhi was and continues to be very controversial, with many critics and opponents both during his lifetime and during the more than six decades since his death. To cite only one famous illustration from Gandhi's lifetime, Winston Churchill, who consistently opposes India's independence from British colonial rule, loathes and has contempt for Gandhi. In 1930

Churchill states: 'It is alarming and also nauseating to see Mr Gandhi, a seditious Middle Temple lawyer, now posing as a fakir of a type well known in the East, striding half-naked up the steps of the Viceregal palace, while he is still organizing and conducting a defiant campaign of civil disobedience, to parley on equal terms with the representative of the King-Emperor.'

Even in India today hundreds of millions of Indians oppose Gandhi and Gandhian approaches. These include 'modern' Westernized Indians, who view Gandhi as irrelevant or a threat to their values and way of life, various religious nationalists and others with religious, caste, class and revolutionary positions rejecting Gandhi's nonviolence and approach to truth and reality.

Who was this M. K. Gandhi, so admired and yet so controversial? When asked about his philosophy and values, Gandhi typically responded with 'my life is my message' and urges others to look at how he lives his life. This is easier said than done.

If you accept the portrayals of Gandhi's youth, primarily drawn from *An Autobiography: The Story of My Experiments with Truth* and other writings, Gandhi's life journey and incredible achievements would seem almost impossible. Based on his descriptions, the Gandhi aged five or ten or even twenty seems to be an unremarkable young person with many personality flaws and limitations. He is of small physical stature and considers himself unathletic and physically weak. Although he is later known for his strict vegetarianism, he becomes convinced in his youth that only eating meat will make Indians strong like the British. And although he is later known for his incredible fearlessness and his view that true nonviolence is impossible without the greatest courage, he is psychologically fearful and repressed as a youth. He is afraid of thieves, ghosts and serpents, and of sleeping in the dark. He is painfully shy, suffers from an immature self-image and has trouble expressing himself. He considers himself a rather mediocre student. If he is later known

Gandhi was the major influence on Martin Luther King Jr's philosophy and methods of nonviolence.

for his remarkable will and incredible self-discipline, self-control and capacity for suffering, he nonetheless describes his youthful unrestrained carnal desires. He often treats his young wife Kasturba badly as he is driven by self-centredness, petulance, unrestrained passions and a domineering attitude.

In short, youthful Gandhi considers himself a rather average, unexceptional person with no obvious talent or potential for greatness. How does this Mohandas Gandhi emerge as one of the most remarkable and most admired human beings of the twentieth century (or of any century)?

M. K. Gandhi usually describes his life and his commitments in simple – often in seemingly oversimplistic – terms. He repeatedly attempts to simplify his lifestyle. In critiquing our modern way of living he urges us to simplify our wants and needs and to recognize that simple living is high living. But when compiling, interpreting and analysing these 'simple' expressions, one uncovers a very complex, nuanced, multidimensional, at times contradictory, open-ended Gandhi, who is continually remaking himself in his ongoing 'experiments with truth'.

Unlike the manner in which many devotees and critics regard him, there is no simple Gandhi blueprint or recipe that we can simply apply to contemporary problems in order to come up with Gandhi answers and solutions. The misleadingly oversimplistic and sometimes false portrayal of Gandhi is evidenced in the well-known inspirational Gandhi quotations that often appear on motivational posters, automobile bumper stickers and greeting cards. One thinks of such citations as 'We must be the change we wish to see in the world'; 'there is enough in the world for everyone's need; there is not enough for everyone's (or anybody's) greed'; 'an eye for an eye ends up making the whole world blind'; and 'God has no religion.' Sometimes one cannot find the precise quotation in any of Gandhi's writings, but it is almost always the case that the attribution is the kind of expression consistent with Gandhi's life and message.

Such a simplistic portrayal is often misleading because it fails to recognize how M. K. Gandhi is contextually engaged and sensitive to changing personal, economic, political, religious and other current issues and crises. He is often full of confusion and doubt, and he struggles to find practical, ethical and spiritual solutions to personal and social problems in his experiments with truth. His action-oriented life and philosophy are realized in practice as expressions of a complex developmental struggle in which he and other imperfect human beings at best move from one limited relative truth to more adequate embodied relative truths.

There may be no famous person of the past century for whom writing about their life, philosophy, significance and legacy poses a greater challenge. Part of the difficulty in reconstructing Gandhi's remarkable life and interpreting and applying his writings arises from very complex relations between texts by and about Gandhi, extremely diverse contexts and a tremendous range of interpretations. Much of this challenge arises from the sheer volume of writings by and about Gandhi. Although he never wrote a lengthy book, Gandhi was a prolific writer, and *The Collected Works of Mahatma Gandhi* comes to a hundred volumes of very diverse and highly fragmented newspaper articles, correspondence, interviews, speeches and other writings.[3]

Gandhi was a very active journalist, and most of the writings in his *Collected Works* are short articles published in the four 'journals' or newspapers that he started and edited: *Indian Opinion*, the English weekly newspaper started by Gandhi in South Africa in 1903 and edited by him until he left South Africa in 1914; *Young India* (the weekly in English) and *Navajivan* (in Gujarati, with later Hindi editions), two newspapers edited by Gandhi in India from 1919 until his imprisonment in 1932; and *Harijan*, the English weekly started by Gandhi in 1933. Along with *Harijan*, Gandhi also started *Harijan Bandu* (in Gujarati) and *Harijan Sevak* (in Hindi) so he could better reach the masses of peasants. It has been estimated that Gandhi wrote more than 80 per cent of the articles in these weekly publications, which he viewed as a major way of communicating with, educating and mobilizing Indians. Gandhi also wrote many letters almost every day to individuals and newspapers.[4]

Much of this challenge in writing about Gandhi also arises from the vast literature of writings about Gandhi.[5] At times it seems that everyone who meets Gandhi feels the need to express some strong view of the encounter. There are words, actions, practices and positions for which Gandhi is given credit or blamed that have more to do with the interpreter than with Gandhi. Descriptions and judgements about Gandhi vary so widely that one often wonders if others are focusing on the same Gandhi and his philosophy. It seems more accurate to interpret such writings about Gandhi as presenting multiple, at times contradictory, M. K. Gandhis and Gandhi theories and practices.

Finally, much of this challenge arises from the incredible range of so many diverse contextual influences in shaping Gandhi's life and message. This can be seen in Gandhi's experiences in Britain and especially in the more than twenty years in South Africa and the more than thirty years after returning to India. In writing about Gandhi's life and message one must necessarily be very selective, omitting what others might find contextually revealing, because Gandhi was engaged in, influenced by and the key influencer of so many complex, meaningful and significant personal, social, local, national and even global and world-historical events. These transformative experiments with nonviolence and truth, arising from Gandhi's contextualized encounters, continue to have great relevance, meaning and significance for major issues of our contemporary world.

While upholding basic ethical and spiritual principles, Gandhi has a remarkable, flexible, open-minded and often changing personality, pursuing truth no matter where it takes him. He is extremely self-critical and continually learning from his 'failed experiments with truth'. He is continually remaking himself, often learning from the transformative process of engaging new contextual influences. In fact, one can make a very good case that the M. K. Gandhi of the 1940s, well into his seventies and up to his assassination, has the greatest personality development, energy, clarity and creativity of his entire lifetime and the most rigorous, developed and adequate understanding of ethical, economic, political, military and other issues. Over the decades Gandhi learns from traditional and modern contexts, from East and West. The Gandhi philosophies and practices that emerge are new, personal, social, local and global. They are neither exclusively Indian nor Western, neither exclusively traditional nor modern, but potentially of greatest importance, relevance and significance for contemporary India and the world.

In short, what makes writing about Gandhi's life and philosophy so challenging is the fact that one can examine the diverse contextual influences, the extensive Gandhi writings and the huge literature about Gandhi and can then reconstruct numerous, complex, at time contradictory M. K. Gandhis and Gandhi philosophies and practices. One can formulate a Gandhi and Gandhi message that are the repressed, reactionary, antimodern expressions of a charlatan, a shrewd and devious politician, a false religious or spiritual manipulator, someone who provided and continues to offer an irrelevant and even disastrous model for India and the world. Or one can formulate a Gandhi and Gandhi message that are the expressions of one of the most ethical and spiritual exemplary human beings who ever lived, whose message is desperately needed economically, socially, politically, culturally, religiously and environmentally, and whose philosophy and practice are of the greatest significance and relevance for the twenty-first century.

In reconstructing the critical life of Mahatma Gandhi and his legacy for the contemporary world, a primary focus will be placed on his central theory and practice of *ahimsa* (not harm, generally translated as Nonviolence and often equated with Love). Gandhi is the best known and most influential proponent of nonviolence of the past century. Martin Luther King Jr, Lech Walesa, César Chávez, Nelson Mandela, Aung San Suu Kyi, the Dalai Lama and many other political and spiritual leaders have acknowledged their indebtedness to the formative example of Gandhi's life and his message of nonviolence. What are the personal and contextual influences that led to Gandhi developing his central commitment to a very broad and deep theory and practice of nonviolence?

M. K. Gandhi gradually develops an ethical and spiritual view of reality that he usually expresses in terms of *satya* (Truth, often equated with God, Self or Soul). How does Gandhi develop such a view of truth, and why does he claim that violence negates and separates us from reality, whereas only nonviolence (often identified with love-force, soul-force and truth-force) allows us to experience reality?

In this regard Gandhi also gradually develops a very critical view of dominant, Western, industrial 'Modern Civilization'. What are the personal and larger contextual influences that allow us to understand how and why Gandhi develops his view of dominant Modern Civilization as violent, exploitative, alienating and a barrier to human development? What are his alternative views and practices of a more ethical, more developed, more civilized way of living based on truth and nonviolence?

Finally, in reconstructing the life of Gandhi and his philosophy, with a central focus on violence and nonviolence, one may submit that his personality as an exemplary ethical model of virtue, character and integrity and his nonviolent message are more relevant, significant and desperately needed today than at any time during his lifetime. As indicated above, one must be selective in focusing on certain contextual influences, personal developments and Gandhi's philosophy and practices. Nevertheless, there is increasing awareness that our modern anti-Gandhi assumptions, values and ways of living our lives are economically unsustainable, environmentally unsustainable and unsustainable in terms of dealing with violence, war, terrorism, exploitation, poverty, racism, sexism, alienation, dehumanization and other forms of humanly caused suffering.

Gandhi's radically different paradigm, his qualitatively different way of being in the world and living his life, may provide the contemporary world with desperately needed alternatives and with some hope for transforming crises that threaten to destroy life on this planet. Gandhi allows us to recognize the dangers of centralized top-down economic, political and military power and the need for greater decentralization and 'self-rule'. He offers us possibilities for nonviolent resistance and constructive alternatives to poverty, inequality, exploitation, oppression, alienation, war, terrorism and other forms of violence. And Gandhi may serve as a catalyst for deepening and broadening our awareness, and challenging us to put into practice qualitatively different views of egalitarianism, democracy, human rights, self-determinism and more nonviolent harmonious relations with other humans, all sentient beings and nature.

Gandhi does not have all of the answers. He was an incredible human being, but he was still human, and had many personality flaws and weaknesses. Many of his views were questionable during his lifetime and have no relevance today. That is why we must be flexible and selective in reconstructing, reinterpreting and reapplying his life and message for the contemporary world. Nevertheless, Gandhi's life, values, philosophy and practices, when reformulated and developed and integrated with compli mentary non-Gandhian approaches, may inspire us and provide invaluable responses in addressing the most pressing crises of the twenty-first century.

1

Youth in India and England

Mohandas Karamchand Gandhi was born on 2 October 1869 in Porbandar, a city on India's western coast on the Arabian Sea, in Kathiawar (or Kathiawad), a peninsula in the state of Gujarat. The Kathiawar Agency was a political unit that was part of the Bombay Presidency in British colonial India. Porbandar was the seat of one of the small princely states of Kathiawar in British India.

Gandhi was born into relative privilege. In terms of the traditional Hindu hierarchical fourfold caste (*varna*) classification (*Brahmins, Khastriyas, Vaishyas* and *Shudras*), he was a member of the *Vaishya* caste of farmers, merchants and businesspeople. In fact the name 'Gandhi' means 'grocer', which apparently had been the family occupation generations earlier. His grandfather, father and uncle served as 'prime ministers' (*Diwans*) to princes of Porbandar and other small Kathiawar states. The Gandhis could be described as middle class and as welcoming diverse cultural and religious experiences.

More specifically, the Gandhis were members of the Hindu Modh community and are identified with the Bania caste or subcaste of merchants, traders and moneylenders. Although Gandhi's ethical, spiritual and political life depart from traditional caste patterns, many have noted his Bania business skills in paying attention to practical details and making practical decisions, carefully arranging his expenditure of time and money, organizing the most detailed matters in his ashrams (his ethical and spiritual residential communities) and other institutions and skilfully raising funds and bargaining and negotiating to resolve conflicts. Most of what we know about Gandhi's youth comes from his *Autobiography*.[1] While very revealing as to Gandhi's self-image and evolving values and priorities, it may be best to take some of his descriptions with a grain of salt. As Gandhi himself states, he does not intend to present a traditional or normal autobiography. He is selective in presenting experiences that make moral and spiritual points and that can serve as lessons for others. In addition Gandhi's autobiography tends to be unbalanced in being extremely self-critical. In fact, throughout his life, he feels the need to share his weaknesses and failed experiments with truth, often not unlike some of the writings in St Augustine's *Confessions*. It is tempting at times to respond, 'don't be so self-critical, you're only a child', 'you're only human', in ways perhaps not unrelated to the severe manner in which Gandhi often treats his four children. Finally, even in Gandhi's writings, one may question whether his portrayal of himself as such a timid, fearful, cowardly, mediocre son and student is completely accurate. For example, the fact that he is so dedicated to nursing his father or that he stands up to and defies his caste elders, who object, threaten and impose severe sanctions on him if he leaves to study law in England, challenges the accuracy of the frequently accepted portrayal of Gandhi's youth as mediocre and cowardly.

Gandhi respects and admires his parents. Mohan's grandfather, Uttamchand Gandhi, was the Diwan of Porbandar, and was succeeded as Diwan by his father, Karamchand Gandhi, called Kaba (1822–1885). Kaba Gandhi was later appointed Diwan of Rajkot and Vankaner districts in Gujarat. Gandhi remembers his father as a person of principle, as truthful, brave, incorruptible, concerned more with virtue than with wealth, but also short-tempered. As with other Hindus in that part of Gujarat, the Gandhis are followers of Lord Vishnu and Gandhi's favourite deity, throughout his life, is Rama, an *avatar* or incarnation of

Gandhi's mother, Putlibai, and father, Karamchand Gandhi.

Vishnu. As a Vaishnava Hindu, Gandhi's father is also very open-minded, tolerant, and respects other cultural and religious approaches. This means that young Gandhi is exposed to many Jains, Parsis, Muslims and others who visit his father's house, and Gandhi repeatedly emphasizes such contextualized experiences as shaping his later pluralistic and inclusive views of religion, politics and culture.

It is for his mother, Putlibai (1822–1891), that Mohan reserves unqualified praise and admiration. She is Karamchand's fourth wife, the first three having died. Mohan is her fourth and youngest child. His older brothers are Laxmidas and Karsandas and his sister is Raliatbehn. Putlibai belongs to the Pranami faith, a Hindu tradition usually associated with Krishna Vaishnava devotion, but which reads the Muslim Qur'an and preaches tolerance and the equality of all religions. Mohan reveres his mother. He describes her as deeply religious, as a saint, with a strong personality and the will to undertake difficult fasts and extreme vows as part of her self-purification. She is a strong role model for Mohan and shapes many of his later ethical and spiritual values and practices. However, it is important to recognize that M. K. Gandhi, even when he goes to England to study law in 1888 aged nineteen, is not particularly knowledgeable about religion in general or Hinduism in particular. In fact he reads and studies his favourite text and 'spiritual guide', the *Bhagavad-Gita*, for the first time when he is in London.

There are several dramatic experiences of an ethical and religious nature in Mohan's childhood. Mohan describes how he is full of fear of ghosts, spirits and the dark, as well as fears that his teachers or other students will criticize or make fun of him. A family servant, a nursemaid named Rambha, comes to his aid by teaching him the *Ramanama*, the repetition of the God Rama's name. This Rama *mantram*, which the mature Gandhi uses as a remedy for the rest of his life, allows him to become increasingly calm and focused, to

Mohandas Gandhi at age 7. This is the earliest photo of Gandhi.

overcome his doubts and fears and feel that God is filling him with strength and direction. It allows him to change what is negative into joyful, fearless, loving, transformative experiences.

Gandhi describes two similar incidents. Although he does not like to read beyond his school assignments, he happens to see his father's copy of *Shravana Pitribhakti Nataka*, a play about Shravana's devotion to his blind parents. He later sees a picture of Shravana carrying his parents. Shravana's devotion and the agonized lament of his parents over his death leave an indelible impression. Similarly, Gandhi is deeply moved by the play *Harishchandra*, with the ideal of a willingness to go through all kinds of ordeals in order to follow the truth.

Here one observes the seeds of later developments in Gandhi's personality, character and commitments. On the one hand, he is a remarkable moralist, always looking for exemplary models of ethical living and character transformation, and courageously following nonviolence and truth wherever they take him. On the other hand, he has limited curiosity and interest in book learning and theory, aesthetic experiences and other worldly phenomena that do not seem to him to have such practical moral and spiritual transformative value. As compared, for example, with Tagore, Gandhi seems to have a narrow, limited focus but, once he becomes convinced of the ethical and spiritual potential of any new contextualized experience, he pursues it with incredible energy, perseverance and creativity.

At the age of six Gandhi enters school in Porbandar, and the next year, when his family moves to Rajkot, he continues his education there through high school. As previously mentioned, Mohan, on the whole, seems to be an unremarkable student, with many fears and other weaknesses, extreme timidity and shyness, no interest in sports and limited intellectual motivation. However, he does have a deep sense of the need to respect his parents, teachers and other elders, and to be honest and to always tell the truth.

As he approaches thirteen Mohan has an arranged marriage to Kasturbai Makanji. A few months older than Mohan, her name is usually shortened to Kasturba (and Kastur) and she is often affectionately named *Ba* (Gujarati 'mother'). Richard Attenborough's remarkable movie, *Gandhi*, which is most responsible for making Gandhi known in the West, provides an idealized view of Gandhi's relationship with Kasturba, with the exception of one very brief scene in South Africa when he angrily drags her from his house after she resists carrying out, emptying and cleaning the chamber pot of a Christian untouchable. Such idealization, with Kasturba's obedience and worship of her husband, is far from the truth. In fact, because of his own later self-criticism and remorse, Gandhi makes outlawing child marriages, as well as the uplifting of the status of women as equal partners, among his major concerns.

Gandhi and Kasturba's long relationship was dynamic and complex, often tumultuous and conflicted, but later evolves into a remarkable partnership. It is not easy being the immature Mohan's child-bride. In oppressive patriarchal ways he is self-centred, extremely insecure and jealous, and assumes that he is the master who can boss his young wife around and control everything she does. He assumes that she is there to be the object of his uncontrolled carnal desires. Even several decades later, when the relationship has matured, Gandhi takes the final vow of *brahmacharya* (usually translated as complete celibacy and chastity, but in a fuller sense, renouncing and controlling all of the ego-desires and passions). It does not seem to have occurred to him that he should have discussed this with his wife beforehand, rather than simply announcing that he informed her of this that day and she accepted it. And, of course, being the wife of the world-famous Mahatma was not always an easy task.

What is remarkable is that the illiterate Kasturba, even as a child-wife, has a strong will and emerges as a remarkable person in her own right. Gandhi develops tremendous admiration for her, even claiming that she is his role model and teacher of *ahimsa*, love and nonviolence, especially since she is able to be patient and firm while undergoing voluntary suffering during the years that he is insensitive and oppressive. Years later, she engages actively in marches and imprisonment and in constructive transformative work. The relationship between Gandhi and Kasturba is closest during the last period of their lives together, and he and numerous others have noted how he is blessed to have had such a patient, strong, virtuous wife, helpmate, comrade and life-partner.

Particularly confusing, and the continuing source of debate, is Gandhi's rather ambiguous relationship with a Muslim youth, Sheikh Mehtab, a friend of Gandhi's older brother Karsan in Rajkot, who focuses on the need to win over and change Mohan.[2] Mehtab is a loose character, with many personality flaws, but Mohan admires his contrasting physical prowess, athletic ability, strength and speed, daring and progressive views on many issues. Gandhi's mother, wife and brother Laxmidas warn him that Mehtab is 'bad company', but Mohan seems dazzled by Mehtab's perceived strengths and claims he is going to reform his weaknesses. The older boy plays on Mohan's cowardly fears, sows seeds of doubt and jealousy about Kasturba, reinforces his sense that he has the right to dominate his wife and takes Mohan to a brothel. The unsettling relationship finally ends decades later in South Africa when Gandhi is called from his law office to find Mehtab with a prostitute in his house.

The best-known incident involving Sheikh Mehtab involves his determination to 'reform' Mohan by getting him to eat meat. Mohan and other students are familiar with Narmad's Gujarati verse: 'Behold the mighty Englishman / He rules the Indian small / Because being a meat-eater / He is five cubits tall.' Mehtab finally convinces Mohan that only by eating meat will he become strong like him, overcome his fears and be able to stand up to the British. At fourteen Mohan finally agrees to commence his goat-eating experiment. He ends the experiment after a year because he decides that lying to his strict vegetarian parents is worse than not eating meat, although he will be able to resume meat-eating after they are no more. Gandhi, so famous for his strict vegetarianism, as an essential part of his nonviolence, was at this point a vegetarian by family and caste inheritance and pressure. Only later, in London, did he become convinced of the health benefits and the ethical, philosophical and spiritual justification of a vegetarian diet.

Mohan describes the dramatic confession of a theft when he is fifteen. For three years, from the time of his wedding until Kaba's death in 1885, Mohan devotes time every day to nursing his sick father, who suffers from a fistula and other painful ailments. Although he describes how such daily nursing denies him the amusements and other aspects of youth, he claims that such selfless service brought him great joy, as it did throughout his later life. Gandhi notes that he would have enjoyed becoming a doctor, but his family and caste prohibited such 'unclean' bodily work and he is steered instead to law.

During this time his brother Karsan incurs a debt, and Mohan clips some gold from an amulet his brother wears in order to clear the debt. Tormented by guilt, Mohan decides to confess the theft of the gold, but he dare not speak to his father. Instead he hands a written confession to Kaba, who is lying on a plank suffering from his fistula. As he describes in his autobiography, Mohan confesses, promises that he will steal no more, asks for forgiveness and punishment and is most concerned that his father will not suffer by punishing himself for his son's wrongdoing. Kaba reads the confession and 'pearl-drops trickled down his cheeks, wetting the paper. For a moment he closed his eyes in thought and then tore up the note.' Mohan, who also cries, can see his father's agony. This leaves an indelible memory. 'Those pearl-drops of love cleansed my heart and washed my sin away.' For Gandhi, this was a lasting memory of pure love and *ahimsa*.

The other dramatic final experience with his father does not leave such a positive memory. Mohan and Kasturba are sixteen and she is pregnant. As Kaba's health greatly deteriorates, Mohan confesses that while he massages his father's legs every night, he is driven by carnal desires and returns immediately to his bedroom. On 'the dreadful night', Kaba's brother Tulsidas offers to relieve Mohan, who accepts the offer, goes straight to his bedroom, and awakens Kasturba. In a few minutes there is a knock on the door and a servant tells Mohan that his father has just died. Rushing back to his father's room, miserable, full of self-blame and shame, Mohan claims that but for his animal passion that blinded him, his father 'would have died in my arms. But now it was my uncle who had had this privilege'. This shame of his lustful carnal desire, even at the hour of his father's death, 'is a blot I have never been able to efface or forget'. His undoubted devotion to his parents 'was weighed and found unpardonably wanting because my mind was at the same moment in the grip of lust'. Gandhi concludes this autobiographical account of his 'double shame' by noting that 'the poor mite that was born to my wife scarcely breathed for more than three or four days. Nothing else could be expected.' As he sometimes does, Gandhi gives a karmic causal relation, attributing such human and even natural disasters to his and other human sins and evil.

The psychologist Erik Erikson and many others focus on this formative traumatic incident in analysing Gandhi's repressed and unhealthy attitude toward sex and other bodily desires.[3] Such explanations are not fully convincing. After all, Kasturba and Gandhi go on to have four sons: Harilal (1888–1948), Manilal (1892–1956), Ramdas (1898–1969) and Devadas (1900–1957); he does not take the *brahmacharya* vow until sixteen years after the incident; he struggles all of his life with his sexual and other desires, and there are many traditional Hindu and other contextual influences that shape his rather ascetic, renunciation approach to

Katurba Gandhi with her four sons in South Africa, 1902.

scx and 'lower', 'animalistic', ego-driven desires. For example, in experimenting with renunciation and taking the *brahmacharya* vow Gandhi is very conscious of his need to control and conserve his sexual and other energies as part of self-purification and to access the maximum focused energy necessary for selfless service in political, social and other struggles.

In 1887 Mohandas passed his matriculation examination in Ahmedabad and entered Samaldas College at Bhavnagar, but he remained in college for only one term. At that time, Mavji Dave, an old family friend and advisor, suggested to the family that Mohandas be sent to England to become a barrister. This appeals to Gandhi and to his family, who are convinced that three years of legal studies in England will then lead to Gandhi's succession to the position of Diwan and to economic success upon his return to India.

There is one big obstacle: in terms of his caste-based Modh Bania community restrictions and his family, especially his mother's, concerns, there is apprehension that a traditional Indian will invariably sin by going abroad. This obstacle is finally overcome when Mohandas agrees to take three sacred vows in the presence of the Jain monk Becharji Swami: not to touch meat, wine and women. His mother then gives her permission. The timid Mohan is remarkably determined and even brave as he defies the caste orders forbidding him from going abroad, even when the caste elders then declare him an outcast and warn that anyone helping him will be subject to fines.

On 4 September 1888, before his nineteenth birthday and shortly after the birth of his first son, Harilal, Gandhi sets sail alone from Bombay to study law at University College, London, reaching the capital on 28 October. His three years studying law to become a barrister that culminate with his being called to the Bar on 10 June 1891 can be seen as a period of considerable transition, personal experimentation and the sowing of seeds that later blossom into his radical transformation. Before coming to England he is a shy timid youth, rarely travels and has very limited intellectual and cultural horizons. In England he encounters new, diverse, challenging contextual situations and has a new freedom, not possible in previous traditional Bania Gujarat contexts, to experiment and gain some greater understanding of who he is and what he believes.

In England Gandhi is for the first time exposed to many Western ethical, social, political, economic, legal and constitutional writings, priorities and values, and experiential ways of being in the world. Many of these he later rejects as false, illusory, superficial, violent, immoral and anti-spiritual, but some of these Western experiences provide him with lasting skills and values, including his critiques of much of traditional hierarchical India. In England he is also exposed, often for the first time, to ideas that later influenced many of his essential ethical and spiritual writings and to his own personal realization of what is of lasting value for him from his own Indian tradition, including his critiques of dominant modernity. What later develops from this initial transitional period and matures in South Africa and in India is Gandhi's new, dynamic, open-ended philosophy and practice, grounded in his commitment to truth and nonviolence. This emerging Gandhi nonviolent paradigm, with its world view and view of human nature and its way of being in the world, will encompass both Western and Indian/Eastern contextual influences and will provide us with challenges and possible solutions allowing us to rethink how we deal with our most pressing contemporary crises.

Gandhi's description of his legal studies is unremarkable. He joins the Inner Temple, one of London's four Inns of Court, to study for the Bar, and although this programme is prestigious, it is not very demanding. What is easily overlooked, especially because of Gandhi's later condemnation of modern Western legal practice as adversarial, violent and divisive, is the invaluable role his British legal training plays in his later life. His legal knowledge and especially his acquired skills are great assets in allowing him to organize nonviolent campaigns, to prepare legal briefs and positions inside and outside the courtroom and to negotiate skilfully in South Africa and in India.

Far more interesting and revealing with regard to the three years in England is what Mohandas experiences outside his legal studies, starting with a brief period of about three months in which he is determined to become a proper English gentleman. English colonial rule gave some Indians the view of English superiority, physical prowess and more advanced civilization, and Gandhi follows a common pattern of trying to mimic an English lifestyle. He buys an expensive tailored suit and a silk top hat, takes lessons in proper elocution, French language, dancing and the violin, and focuses on changing his physical appearance. Largely because he cannot afford such an expensive lifestyle and feels awkward and unfulfilled by these changes he gives up on this experiment. He commits himself to being a student and he begins to experiment with a less expensive, simplified, more self-sufficient lifestyle that includes long walks and vegetarian dietetic experiments. During his years in England, despite temptations and a few close calls, he manages to uphold his three vows of not touching meat, alcohol or women.

The two most interesting features of Gandhi's experiences in England focus on vegetarianism and religion. Upholding his vegetarian vow, he struggles with his diet before finding vegetarian restaurants in London. He begins reading books on vegetarianism, becomes active in the London Vegetarian Society, gets to know leading vegetarian authors and activists, contributes articles to the society's magazine, *The Vegetarian*, and takes somewhat of a leadership role. At first Mohandas, who has been vegetarian by family and caste inheritance and not by personal choice, is mainly attracted to the health benefits of a vegetarian diet. He then develops an ethical, philosophical and religious understanding and commitment. He begins to experiment with different kinds of vegetarian diets and this becomes a lifelong commitment. His vegetarianism, as an essential part of the need to control his palate and food consumption, becomes a key for Gandhi's self-purification and realization of reality through nonviolent truthful living.

Although Mohandas had been raised in a tolerant and open-minded home, he really knows very little about his own Hinduism or other religions. Two theosophists, the Keightley brothers, ask

Gandhi, front right, with members of the Vegetarian Society, London, 1890.

Gandhi's help with reading the *Bhagavad-Gita*. Although the *Gita* becomes his favourite text and his ethical and spiritual manual for daily living, he had never previously read it. He joins the Keightleys in reading Edwin Arnold's translation, *The Song Celestial*, and uses his limited knowledge of Sanskrit to work with the original. The brothers then tell him of Arnold's *The Light of Asia* on the Buddha, and he reads this with even greater interest.

For the first time Gandhi begins to study Christianity and other religions. Earlier he had a negative view of intolerant, exclusive, judgemental Christian missionaries who attack Hindus as sinful idol worshippers. The theosophists he meets seem to respect all religions, including Hinduism, and his closest Christian contacts, many of whom are committed vegetarians, present a more appealing version of Christianity. He is urged to read the Bible and reading the New Testament's Sermon on the Mount especially moves him.

These new transitional experiences shape Gandhi's later views of the underlying unity and equality of all religious paths and the fact that all organized religions express both lofty ethical and spiritual teachings and also the impurities of intolerance, hatred, oppression and violence. These experiences begin a process in which Gandhi identifies with nonviolence, tolerance, unifying interrelatedness and other principles and values he considers most worthy in his Hinduism, while criticizing and reforming its many impurities. With regard to Christianity, Gandhi begins to appreciate and embrace Christian values, as seen in the Sermon on the Mount, the exemplary model of a selfless, loving, voluntarily suffering, nonviolent Jesus, and various interpretations, especially as presented in the writings of Leo Tolstoy. What is also fascinating is how various Christians are attracted to Gandhi, whether the Baptist minister Joseph Doke in South Africa, his first biographer, the Anglican priest Charles Andrews, one of his closest associates in South Africa and India, or the many who see Gandhi as the most Christ-like human being of their times or of any time during the past 2,000 years.

Two days after being called to the Bar, Gandhi sails for India on 12 June 1891. Upon his arrival home, he receives the 'severe shock', more painful than his father's death, that his beloved mother had died while he was abroad. His family had attempted to protect him from the suffering by withholding the news until his return.

Gandhi applies for admission to the Bombay High Court but his legal practice in Rajkot and Bombay is very disappointing. Lacking knowledge of Indian law and still tormented with personal timidity and insecurity he becomes known as a 'briefless barrister'. Although he was challenged and grew through his transitional experiences in England, his life at this point has no real direction and there is no indication of a successful legal career in India.

What occurs to transform so radically this rather unremarkable youth and young lawyer, with no obvious potential for future greatness, into the larger-than-life Mahatma, the most influential proponent of nonviolence in the contemporary world?

2

South Africa

In so many ways Gandhi's South Africa experiences represent the decisive turning point in his life. No one would have been more surprised than M. K. Gandhi, who accepts a rather minor role in a legal case in South Africa that is supposed to take him away from India for not more than a year. Instead he remains for 21 years, although the total time is closer to 19, since it includes two extended trips to India and two to England.

The Gandhi who leaves Bombay on 19 April 1893 and arrives in Port Durban on 23 May has no clear direction and is unsure of who he is and what he believes. He has had an unsuccessful beginning to a legal career. He dresses in expensive Western suits and wears a stylish turban. Although he is an unknown, insignificant Indian, this Gandhi, so unlike the later Gandhi, is self-centred with a rather elitist pride in the fact that he is a British-educated barrister. He is a rather anglicized Indian and considers himself a very loyal citizen of the British Empire, with its advanced modern civilization.

The Gandhi who leaves South Africa for the last time on 18 July 1914 emerges as the Indian leader in South Africa, known and admired in India, with a strong commitment to the philosophy and practices of truth and nonviolence. He is the originator and organizer of mass, moral, nonviolent, activist, *satyagraha* campaigns of noncooperation, resistance and civil disobedience. He is the leader who boldly negotiates with the most powerful authorities,

As a barrister practicing law in Johannesburg, 1906.

is self-confident and self-reliant and endures voluntary and involuntary suffering and imprisonment. He is the remarkable person who remakes himself in appearance, diet and ways of living and rejects much of the modern Western civilization he had embraced. In short, the Mohandas Gandhi who leaves South Africa for the final time looks like the Indian leader and world famous Mahatma, the most influential proponent of nonviolence. How does this radical transformation occur?[1]

What is the South African context within which Indians live in the late nineteenth century? As becomes legally transparent in later Apartheid laws, there are four main racial groupings: the dominant Whites (mainly the minority privileged British and the larger number of Dutch Boers or Afrikaners), the majority Blacks or indigenous tribal Africans, the 'coloured' or 'mixed' population and the Indians. The Indians come after 1860 as indentured servants to work on the sugar plantations and later as merchants and traders. Gandhi lives in the eastern coastal state of Natal, a British Crown Colony that includes Durban, and the interior state of Transvaal, the Boer territory that includes Pretoria and Johannesburg. Upon arrival he is immediately aware of the strong anti-Indian race prejudice, oppression and humiliation, as seen in how Whites address Indians, including Gandhi, with the insulting epithets 'coolie' (a pejorative term for Asian labourers) and 'Sammy' (or 'Sami', a derogative term derived from the fact that many Indians have 'swamy' as part of their last names, though the term in India means 'master' or 'guru').

As Gandhi describes in his autobiography and in his book *Satyagraha in South Africa*, a Meman Muslim firm in Porbandar, Dada Abdullah & Co., writes to his brother Laxmidas, asking if Mohandas would be willing to go to South Africa to assist in a lawsuit. The firm does a lot of business in South Africa and the wealthy head there is Abdullah Sheth. A directionless and desperate Mohandas agrees to take this rather minor case in which

Abdullah files a financial claim against his relative Tyeb Sheth, who lives in Pretoria, where the case will be heard.

What is most significant about this case is what it reveals about Gandhi's developing values that go far beyond his legal career and extend to his entire philosophy and practices of nonviolence and truth. Gandhi is successful in winning the case before an arbitrator. He is disturbed when he realizes that in the present adversarial legal system the lawyer who 'wins' most decisively, who destroys the opponent as legal enemy, who secures the maximum financial settlement, is the most successful. For Gandhi, this is an aggressive violent approach that often opportunistically conceals and distorts morality and truth and that stirs up and leads to bitterness, hatred, desire for revenge and escalating violence. Gandhi convinces Abdullah that he should not bankrupt and humiliate his relative and should accept smaller settlement payments over a longer period of time. For Gandhi this illustrates the only justifiable role for a lawyer (as for a doctor, journalist, politician and other 'professionals'): to live a life of selfless service, pursuing truth and justice and always aiming for a win–win resolution of conflicts. In such conflict resolution, you relate to 'the other' not as enemy to be exploited and dominated, but instead as an integral part of your nonviolent, loving, truthful, interconnected, unifying ethical and spiritual reality.

On the seventh or eighth day after his arrival in South Africa, Gandhi experiences the following famous incident at Pietermaritzburg, popularly known as Maritzburg, the capital and second largest city of Natal (now the province of Kwazulu-Natal). This experience is sometimes described as the most decisive transformative turning point in Gandhi's life.

As befitting his self-image of a British-trained barrister, M. K. Gandhi has a first-class train ticket for his journey from Durban to Pretoria. A white passenger complains, and Gandhi is asked by an official to move from the first-class compartment to a van

With two of his closest associates in South Africa, his devoted secretary Sonia Schlesin and Henry Polak, in front of his law office in Johannesburg, 1905.

compartment. When he refuses a police constable is summoned and throws Gandhi and his luggage off the train at Pietermaritzburg railway station. Humiliated, huddled and shivering throughout the night in the unlit waiting room, Gandhi debates whether to return to India or remain in South Africa. He resolves that the former would be cowardly and that it is his duty to remain in order to finish his legal case, expose colour prejudice and fight for his rights.

He reaches Charlestown, where he continues his journey by stagecoach, experiencing more race prejudice, insults and humiliation. Although he has a valid ticket, the driver refuses to allow him to sit inside with whites and Gandhi reluctantly agrees to sit outside next to the driver. Later the driver places a dirty sackcloth on the footboard and orders Gandhi to get down and sit there. When Gandhi refuses, he starts beating him and dragging him down. Fortunately some of the alarmed white passengers intervene and say that he can sit inside with them. There are other similar humiliating experiences in Gandhi's introduction to South Africa, such as being ordered in court to remove his turban, and rather than experience the humiliation he decides to leave. On another occasion a guard on duty by President Kruger's house in Pretoria pushes and kicks him from the footpath into the street.

The Pietermaritzburg railway station incident, reinforced by similar experiences, marks the beginning of a new and radically different Gandhi, even if it takes years and decades for the transformation to mature. Responding to race prejudice and humiliation, Gandhi begins to evolve as a human being with a new self-confidence and determination, an awareness of the violence of injustice and inequality, a sensitivity to moral and spiritual duty, a commitment to a life of nonviolent dignity, freedom and integrity that involves selfless service encompassing the well-being of others.

His case concluded, Gandhi is about to return to India when he learns of a bill that will disenfranchise Natal Indians and is 'the first nail in our coffin'. Persuaded to remain, Gandhi increasingly identifies with the plight of South African Indians, keeps extending his stay and emerges as the Indian leader. In 1894 he becomes founder-secretary of the Natal Indian Congress. Over the years he focuses almost entirely on the living conditions of Indians and on race prejudice and oppression directed against the Indian community. He becomes aware of and resists blatant

With co-founders of the Natal Indian Congress, Durban, 1895.

injustices denying civil and human rights as expressed through anti-Indian legislation that involves disenfranchisement, unjust and unbearable taxation, removing the legitimacy of Hindu, Muslim and other Indian marriages, and humiliating racial group registration. On at least two occasions he is almost killed and in 1908 he begins the first of his many imprisonments. In all, including the later imprisonments in India, Gandhi will spend about six years in prison.

Gandhi starts *Indian Opinion* in 1903, communicates and interacts with influential leaders in India, such as his 'political guru' Gopal Krishna Gokhale, Sir Pherozeshah Mehta and Bal Gangadhar 'Lokmanya' Tilak, as well as leaders in Britain and South Africa. He develops skills in symbolically representing and publicizing injustices and in organizing nonviolent campaigns. He experiments with personal and group living, including taking the vow of *brahmacharya* in 1906 and founding the Phoenix Settlement ashram outside Durban in 1904 and the Tolstoy Farm ashram outside Johannesburg in 1910. He experiments with undermining hierarchical distinctions and prohibitions, including those involving manual labour, caste and untouchability, with simple living, alternative medical and health practices and alternative food consumption that involves a radical vegetarian diet. By 1912 he completely rejects European dress.

Although Gandhi is very limited and selective in his reading, there are at least three dramatic, life-changing influences that arise from the literature he reads in South Africa. In this regard he lists Leo Tolstoy's *The Kingdom of God is Within You*, John Ruskin's *Unto This Last* and the Jain Rajchandra (Shrimad Raychandbhai Ravajibhai Mehta), who comes closest to being Gandhi's religious mentor or guru, as the three most important modern influences on his life.

Gandhi writes that Tolstoy's *The Kingdom of God is Within You* 'overwhelmed' him and 'left an abiding impression'. He even claims

Drawing of Gandhi in prison in South Africa, 1908.

that it is reading Tolstoy that converts him to a philosophy and practice of nonviolence.[2] Tolstoy is critical of traditional organized, coercive, violent religion. He submits that we should instead follow the divine within each of us, focusing on our inner experiences that constitute a meaningful ethical and spiritual existence. His focus is on the example of Jesus Christ in the Gospels, especially in the Sermon on the Mount. We should embody the principle of 'non-resistance' to violence and evil, in the sense of turning the other cheek, not hating or killing and loving our enemies. Gandhi corresponds with Tolstoy late in his life. He obtains permission to translate and publish Tolstoy's *A Letter to a Hindoo*, which claims that weak Hindus and other Indians, who are 99 per cent of the population, are complicit with and largely responsible for their own enslavement by a small number of British colonialists. They can free themselves if they adopt nonviolence and nonviolent noncooperation with evil. All of these principles from Tolstoy are embraced by Gandhi and become major features of his philosophy and practices of nonviolence.

In a dramatic description Gandhi tells how reading Ruskin's *Unto This Last*, on a train trip from Johannesburg to Durban in 1904, has a 'magical influence' on him and is a 'turning point' in his life.[3] Gandhi cannot lay the book aside, gets no sleep, discovers some of his deepest convictions in the book and 'is determined to change my life in accordance with the ideals of the book'. Ruskin's teachings that Gandhi embraces are that 'the good of the individual is contained in the good of all', that all labour 'has the same value' in that 'all have the same right of earning their livelihoods from their work' and a life of labour, as involving farming and handi-crafts, 'is the life worth living'. After reading *Unto This Last* Gandhi founds his intentional community at the Phoenix Settlement, and this serves as the model for his other ashrams. He later publishes the Gujarati translation of *Unto This Last* as *Sarvodaya*, meaning 'the welfare of all', and that is the name of Gandhi's economic philosophy. One cannot overestimate the formative influence of Ruskin's *Unto This Last* in shaping Gandhi's challenging and innovative philosophy of nonviolence with his emphasis on meeting the basic material needs of others, focusing on those who are most exploited and with greatest need, and formulating a social relational approach that is egalitarian and recognizes the contributions and value of all labour. This economic philosophy allows Gandhi to oppose hierarchical, dominant, modern economic systems as inherently exploitative and violent.

The third influential source of literature can be described as Gandhi's interest in religious writings. Much of the impetus for this comes from other believers in South Africa. Some are confrontational in a judgemental, intolerant and verbally violent way, and this reinforces Gandhi's aversion to traditional organized religion and its aggressive missionaries. Others approach Gandhi in a respectful and loving way in their attempts at interesting him in and or even converting him to their religions. At their urging Gandhi studies the Bible, the Qur'an and other religious scriptures and writings.

Gandhi becomes confused and, at a time of doubt and crisis, turns to the Jain Rajchandra, whom he knew as a family friend in Gujarat. Rajchandra, who dies at the age of 33, is known as a philosopher, poet, jeweller and person of spotless character with a remarkable sense of detachment, equanimity and renunciation. Gandhi is impressed with his burning desire for self-realization and his central 'passion to see God face to face'. Rajchandra has a scholarly knowledge and respect for Hinduism. In 1894 Gandhi sends him 28 questions and receives appreciated answers and recommended readings and guidance on Hinduism, including extolling the pure path of *brahmacharya*. Gandhi states that of all the religious leaders and teachers he met, he most respects Rajchandra, although he could not accept him or anyone else as his spiritual guru.[4]

These experiences point to the importance of diverse contextual influences in negatively and positively shaping Gandhi's unique approach to God, Hinduism and other religions. Under the influence of Tolstoy, Rajchandra and others, Gandhi, for example, repeatedly claims that he embraces Christ, especially the essential teaching as symbolically represented by Christ on the Cross, as expressed in the Sermon on the Mount, but he doesn't like what traditional Christians do. He claims to accept the essential Christian message while rejecting Christ as the Son of God and exclusive divine incarnation, and he claims that it would not matter to the ethical and spiritual teaching whether Christ had never lived. When asked by Christians why he doesn't become a Christian, he responds: 'What makes you think I'm not?' And he provides similar responses to other religions. He can affirm that he is a Muslim, and that the splendid Qur'an contains as much, but not more, truth as the Vedas, Bible and other scriptures. He then goes on to tell Muslims, as well as other believers, that their sacred scriptures are human constructions and that they should reject anything in their religious texts and institutions that violates their own moral experiences and human reason.

Similarly, increasingly reacting to British, Christian and other condemnations in South Africa, Gandhi becomes comfortable affirming that he is a proud Indian and a believing Hindu. But he is critical of much of traditional Hinduism, scriptural claims, hierarchical institutions and violent practices. His emerging sense of nonviolent Hinduism has a strong sense of renunciation, of a rather stoic asceticism, of self-control of ego-desires and attachments as part of self-purification. But his Hindu approach rejects traditional Hindu renunciation of an illusory world. His nonviolent, truthful, moral approach is very worldly, and his renunciation focuses on how we engage in transformative action and service.

While in South Africa Gandhi's changing approaches to war are striking, puzzling and often controversial. He repeatedly affirms his nonviolent philosophy that war is immoral. However, in 1899 he organizes and leads a volunteer Indian Ambulance Corps in the Boer War on the side of the British, even though he claims that his sympathies lie with the Dutch Afrikaners. Even more troubling, in 1906 he organizes and leads a volunteer Ambulance Corps of Indian stretcher-bearers in the 'Zulu Rebellion' on the side of the British, even though he writes that his sympathies are with the native Zulus. When carrying wounded Zulus on stretchers he is particularly disturbed, especially by how the British cruelly inflict mass slaughter as more of a manhunt than a war. What makes his involvement even more controversial arises from his statements about Zulus and other indigenous Africans that strike many as uninformed, condescending and racist.

In justifying his participation in the Boer War and Zulu Rebellion Gandhi's major justification is that this is his duty as a loyal supporter of the British Empire. His other major justification is that the British consider Indians weak, cowardly, backward and incapable of self-governance. He believes that volunteering in the British war effort will change British attitudes, demonstrating that

With the Indian Ambulance Corps during the Boer War in South Africa, 1899–1900. Gandhi is fifth from the left in the middle row.

Indians are loyal, courageous and worthy of respect. This may contribute to India's growing movement for greater self-rule and independence. Of course, the latter leaves Gandhi open to the charge that, in a seemingly anti-Gandhian manner, he is willing to sacrifice the lives of Boers and Zulus in order to achieve Indian ends. Such opportunism blatantly violates Gandhi's major philosophical doctrine that ends, even noble ends, cannot be used to justify immoral violent means.

In 1914, after he leaves South Africa, Gandhi supports the British war effort by raising an ambulance corps in London. In 1918 he actively recruits in India for the British war effort. Many of his closest associates are confused and dismayed. They do not understand how M. K. Gandhi, the opponent of war and violence, can justify such a position.

Gandhi is a remarkable human being, but one who is contextually shaped and has many personal weaknesses. What is remarkable is his capacity to be self-critical and to transform himself. In the illustrations of his approach to war and in many other examples, the later Gandhi often rejects earlier positions in terms of his evolving philosophy and practices.

Three South African experiences of monumental significance demonstrate this evolution in transformation in Gandhi, his philosophy and his influence: first, the gathering in 1906 in Johannesburg that leads to the introduction of *satyagraha*; second, the writing of *Hind Swaraj* in 1909 on the return ship from London, and third, the later *satyagraha* struggles, culminating in the 'Great March' of 1913.

On 11 September 1906 a packed gathering assembles at the Empire Theatre in Johannesburg to protest a Transvaal Asiatic Department's proposal to amend the Asiatic Law. This law will require Indians to obtain new certificates of registration, be fingerprinted and produce the certification each time it is requested by police officers, who will be allowed to enter private houses for inspection. Failure to comply would invite fines, imprisonment or deportation. After speakers support a resolution opposing the proposed law, Haji Habib dramatically asserts that the oppositional resolution must be passed 'with God as witness' and 'in the name of God that he would never submit to that law'. Deeply impressed, Gandhi proposes that Transvaal's Indians consider taking such a solemn pledge, and as he describes in *Satyagraha in South Africa,* 'all present, standing with upraised hands, took an oath with God as witness not to submit'. This is usually dated as the beginning of Gandhi's *satyagraha,* his revolutionary approach and best-known method for implementing his philosophy of non-violence. Dissatisfied with the passive nature and other connotations of the commonly used term 'passive resistance', Gandhi offers a prize in *Indian Opinion,* and in 1907 he modifies the winning entry to '*satyagraha*' ('firmness for the truth', translated as truth-force, love-force and soul-force).

Two years later Gandhi goes to London during July–November in an unsuccessful attempt to lobby against anti-Indian legislation and for South African Indian interests. On his return voyage he writes *Hind Swaraj* in only ten days, 13–22 November, and also translates Tolstoy's 'A Letter to a Hindoo'. Gandhi scholars and followers often describe *Hind Swaraj* as his most important work.[5]

More of a manifesto, an argument, an invitation to rethink values, approaches and philosophies than a scholarly book, the 90-page *Hind Swaraj* takes the form of a dialogue between the Editor, expressing Gandhi's views, and the Reader, representing various prominent Indian views, including those of expatriates Gandhi has met in London. The Reader consists of privileged moderates, including leaders in the Indian National Congress, who believe that Indian independence can be achieved through legal reforms and constitutional means, and extremists, including anarchists and terrorists, who believe that Indian independence can be achieved only by using any means necessary, including illegal, extra-constitutional and violent means.

Hind Swaraj is especially significant because it reveals the radical changes Gandhi has undergone in South Africa. Often in misleadingly oversimplistic and irrelevant ways, it presents profound insights, values and commitments that are at the foundation of Gandhi's mature philosophy and practices and may be very relevant today. He forcefully argues that Indians should stop worshipping and imitating some supposedly superior British and Western Civilization. According to Gandhi, true civilization and culture have to do with how human beings live their lives in the world. 'Modern Civilization' is violent, materialist, consumerist, ego-centered, focuses on bodily desires and privileges the 'machine craze'. It is alienating, dehumanizing and lacks any deep sense of morality and duty. The superior 'Ancient Civilization' of India is human-centric rather than machine-centric and money-centric. It is essentially nonviolent, privileges morality and spiritual realization, addresses our higher human capacities and focuses on human integrity and harmonious relations with other beings and with nature.

More specifically, in terms of the book's title, Gandhi submits that both the moderates and the extremists uphold a limited and false view of _swaraj_. They mimic the inadequate methods, values, and models from 'Modern Civilization'. Even the so-called radical approaches of the extremists simply embrace modern colonial values they claim to reject. They only wish to exchange the violent British tiger for a violent Indian tiger, which will perpetuate the domination and exploitation of most Indians. Instead Gandhi proposes something far more revolutionary: real political independence, not realized in Britain, the USA or India in 1947, is based on real 'self-rule' (_swa_ = self and _raj_ = rule). Without citizens capable of self-rule, actively participating and self-determining, we cannot experience the real egalitarianism, freedom and democracy extolled, but not realized, in 'independent' modern nation states.

Gandhi during the *satyagraha* campaign in South Africa, 1913.

Therefore during his final years in South Africa M. K. Gandhi develops a more authentic understanding of who he is, what he believes and how to put this into practice through innovative experiments with truth, especially through heightened and broadened *satyagraha* campaigns. These include methods of nonviolent resistance, picketing, burning registration cards, civil disobedience and arrests. Traditional Indian class and gender restrictions are broadened so that *satyagraha* can include women, poor mineworkers and their families. These experiments culminate in what Gandhi and others call the 'Great March' of April 1913, consisting of 2,037 men, 127 women and 57 children, from Natal and crossing the Transvaal Volksrust border. For this last and most successful South African resistance campaign Gandhi and the *satyagrahis* focus on the anti-Indian tax, refusal to recognize Indian marriages that are not Christian unions, immigration restrictions and indentured labour. Police brutality, killings and arrests lead to pressure on the South African Government from London and Delhi. This leads to the agreement between General Jan Smuts and Gandhi and the passage of the Indians' Relief Act of 1914. The tax is abolished, Indian marriages are recognized as legal and various rights and the easing of some entry restrictions are granted.

Gandhi sees this victory, albeit a limited one, as the culmination of the long *satyagraha* struggle that started in September 1906, and he decides that it is time to return to India. The Gandhi who enters South Africa in expensive suits and fights to travel first class leaves as the Gandhi who dresses like a poor indentured labourer and travels by the lowest third class. But the unknown Indian has become the widely recognized and admired leader, the proponent of love and nonviolence and author of the revolutionary method of mass nonviolent resistance and transformation. On 18 July 1914 the Gandhis leave Cape Town for England, and on 19 December they set sail for Bombay.

3

From the Return to India to the Salt March

Well-known images and stereotypes of M. K. Gandhi are usually drawn from the last 33 years of his life, which was spent almost entirely in India. Both admirers and critics often focus on one of two oppositional portrayals. Is Gandhi a politician or a religious figure? On the one hand, Gandhi is the spiritual leader, mystical ascetic and religious believer of deep faith. For many admirers he is morally and spiritually so far ahead of his time, too good for this world and ultimately martyred. For many critics he's a religious charlatan, exploiting his charisma and obscurantist religious authority. On the other hand, Gandhi is the skilful politician, the political leader in India's struggle for independence and the proponent of a revolutionary nonviolent political vision and method. For many admirers he offers the best hope for a new moral and spiritual way of political engagement that is urgently needed for resolving violent conflicts, terrorism and war. For many critics he is a reactionary, anti-modern, irrelevant politician, who is a shrewd and unscrupulous manipulator and mixes religion with politics in irrational and dangerous ways.

Gandhi's life provides considerable evidence, when abstracted and taken out of overall context, to substantiate both images. But neither portrayal of Gandhi in India, the admired or criticized political or religious figure, is fully justified. Gandhi certainly considers himself deeply religious but he is not a traditional religious figure and he rarely identifies with organized institutionalized religion.

Indeed, although Gandhi often makes religious appeals, an open-minded ethical atheist or nonreligious person can easily relate to most of Gandhi's writings and practices, including most references to 'God' who is usually interchangeable with 'morality'. Gandhi certainly considers himself deeply political but he is not a traditional politician and usually avoids organized political institutions. For Gandhi, any worthy religious approach must be political since it must be concerned with poverty, oppression, exploitation and injustice. For Gandhi, any worthy political approach must religious in the sense that it must be guided by moral and spiritual visions and methods.

The religious and the political, while complementary integral parts of a whole way of being in the world and necessary for restricting and transforming the dangerous tendencies of each by itself, always present a kind of tension in Gandhi's life, philosophy and practices. Because of the religious–political tension and oscillations, Gandhi often bewilders, subverts and infuriates both supporters and critics as, for example, when he dramatically inserts some moral or spiritual stand in the midst of practical political negotiations and campaigns or when he dramatically inserts some political stand that challenges traditional hierarchical religious discourse and contextualized institutions.

The shifting political–spiritual distinction is valuable for viewing Gandhi's last 33 years in India. There are periods in which Gandhi's focus is on the major political work of *satyagraha* campaigns, political writings and negotiations, doing political research, working with leaders of the Indian National Congress, organizing noncooperation and civil disobedience, going to prison, and political work dominates his life. There are other periods, such as 1922–8 or the mid to late 1930s, in which Gandhi consciously withdraws from active political life and focuses on self-purification, ashram life, constructive work, and 'nonpolitical' ethical and spiritual work dominates his life.

The two major concepts or principles in Gandhi's philosophy are *satya* (truth, God, being, reality) and *ahimsa* (nonviolence, love, benevolent harmlessness). The two major ways of implementing truth and nonviolence are through *satyagraha* (truth-force, soul-force, love-force) and constructive work, as formulated in Gandhi's Constructive Programme. It is misleading, as is sometimes presented, to view *satyagraha* campaigns as political and constructive work campaigns as moral and spiritual. For Gandhi the two are inseparable dialectical parts of the whole. *Satyagraha*, for example, is not simply nonviolent resistance, but is always grounded in and a way of realizing positive moral and spiritual values. Constructive work, as in dealing with problems of poverty and patriarchy and caste oppression, is necessarily political. Nevertheless, there is a valuable distinction of emphasis in Gandhi's life after returning to India. When he emphasizes *satyagraha* campaigns, public political organizing, negotiating and struggle dominate his life. When he emphasizes moral and spiritual constructive work, which he says is the life he prefers, he often withdraws from active political engagement.

When Gandhi returns to India he faces several daunting problems. He has no clear direction and feels that he really does not know India. He accepts Gokhale's advice that he should spend the next year staying out of the public light and getting to know the real India. Although the challenges in South Africa were daunting, in many ways, they were relatively easy compared to what Gandhi faces in India. In South Africa he had much more freedom to experiment than he would have enjoyed in traditional India. The Indian community was modest in size, rather homogeneous, and the Hindus and Muslims Gandhi knew managed to avoid communal religious conflicts. India, by way of contrast, has over 300 million people, most of whom are isolated illiterate village peasants, with no unifying national structure or organization and with endless caste, class, religious, ethnic, linguistic, regional and other divisions. Divided Indians are rendered even more powerless as the most prized jewel in the crown of British colonial divide-and-rule domination and exploitation.

Perhaps the most daunting challenge Gandhi faces is that there are no existing models, structures, organizations or institutions in India to accommodate his emerging philosophy and practices. His approach is remarkably innovative, challenging, and sometimes baffling. He appropriates symbols, values, teachings and practices from traditional India, but he is not a traditional Indian. He appropriates what he finds valuable from the modern West, but he is not an Indian modernist. What is truly astounding in light of these challenges is that, within four years of his return to India, this Gandhi, increasingly confident of the truth of his nonviolent philosophy and methods, emerges as the best-known and most influential leader in India.

Gandhi reaches India on 9 January 1915 and on 25 May he founds Satyagraha Ashram at Kochrab village near Ahmedabad in Gujarat. In the middle of 1917, after the outbreak of plague, he shifts to the banks of the Sabarmati River near Ahmedabad, and he is the leader of the Sabarmati Ashram until the Salt Satyagraha in 1930. At the ashrams he experiments with vows and practices involving nonviolence, truth, respect for all faiths, nonpossession, simple living, celibacy, *swadeshi* (self-sufficient economy based on one's local or national products), removal of untouchability and other attempts at constructive work of moral and spiritual regeneration.

In 1917 Gandhi is invited by farmer Rajkumar Shukla to come to the aid of the impoverished suffering peasants of Champaran in north Bihar. The planters, primarily British, require peasants to grow indigo that is no longer profitable and to make cash payments or pay increased rent. Champaran becomes Gandhi's first *satyagraha* in India. His method is to do a careful investigation, with interviews and the accumulation of data, so that he can provide an 'ocular demonstration' of the grave injustices and suffering. He then tries to remove the injustice through negotiations before resorting to nonviolent resistance and civil disobedience. He is successful: the demands for compulsory growing of indigo and required cash payments are abolished. Champaran Satyagraha starts to build Gandhi's reputation and allows him to begin his increasing identification with Indian peasants and with all who suffer most and are most oppressed. It is an illustration of individual *satyagraha*.[1]

In 1918 he is invited by Anasuya Sarabhai, the daughter of a wealthy mill-owner and philanthropist, who is organizing textiles labour along Gandhi lines, to intervene in a strike of Ahmedabad textiles workers demanding higher wages from the mill-owners. Gandhi sides with the workers, tries to establish harmonious relations between them and the owners and, for the first time in a nonviolent struggle, undertakes a fast. This leads to arbitration and an increase in wages. Later in 1918 Gandhi participates in the Kaira Satyagraha (also known as the Kheda Satyagraha), a tax revolt led and organized by Sardar Vallabhbhai Patel, a close Gandhi associate and leader in the freedom movement. In desperate straits after the failure of their crops, the peasants in the Kaira district of Gujarat in the Bombay Presidency rather impressively demand the suspension of land revenue assessments and finally achieve some relief.

These small local campaigns set the stage for Gandhi's first national *satyagraha* in 1919. The British, without consulting Indians, publish the unpopular Rowlatt Bills in February 1919. Formulated to suppress Indian anti-colonial terrorism and revolt, the bills, which become law on 18 March, greatly restrict free speech and civil liberties. Gandhi launches the Rowlatt Satyagraha, with a pledge to disobey the law, mass demonstrations and a surprisingly effective *hartal* (mass protest marked by strike action with cessation of work). British responses include violent repression.

One of the best-known incidents of overt British violence occurs during this period. On 13 April 1919, under the orders of Brigadier-General Reginald Dyer, armed troops fire on innocent Indians who have assembled in peaceful protest. Dyer justifies the Jallianwalla Bagh Massacre, also known as the Amritsar Massacre, as necessary to teach Indians a lesson. The mass slaughter results in the killing of 378 and the injury of over 1,500 Indians. Gandhi is shocked by the slaughter and the British response, including widespread sympathy in England for Dyer's position. After observing examples of sporadic Indian violence, Gandhi concludes that it was a 'Himalayan miscalculation' on his part to think that Indians are sufficiently prepared and committed for mass nonviolent resistance. He suspends the national *satyagraha* on 18 April.

The Amritsar Massacre and other examples of British violence produce a significant change in Gandhi's attitude and approach: British claims now increasingly appear false, immoral and hypocritical. India, not Britain, has the moral high ground, and Gandhi sees the need to end British rule and break with the Empire. This becomes clear in the more ambitious Non-Cooperation Campaign of 1920–22.

The idea of *swaraj* spreads throughout India and in 1920 Gandhi dramatically announces that India can attain national independence within one year through mass nonviolent means. The Indian National Congress unanimously adopts Gandhi's resolution to this effect in December. Congress is transformed into a mass organization with Gandhi as its leader. Gandhi relates to the Indian masses, raises issues of poverty and the need for the *charka* (spinning-wheel), which he has placed on the *swaraj*-flag. On 31 July 1921 he calls for the boycott of foreign cloth and arranges for such clothes to be discarded through a huge bonfire in Bombay. On 21 September, in Madurai, in solidarity with the poorest of the poor, he discards his remaining attire, shaves his head and wraps himself in the *khadi* (homespun) loincloth.

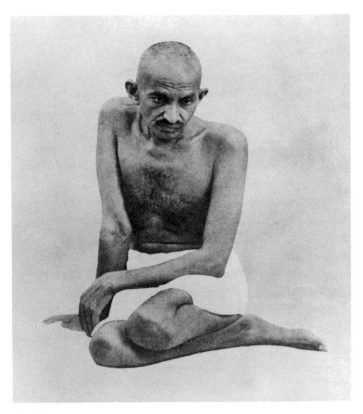
Gandhi in 1924.

Nonviolent revolution, using resistance and civil disobedience,
seems imminent, and Congress delegates sole executive authority
to Gandhi.

There are outbreaks of some Indian violence, and on 5 February
1922 Gandhi is informed of mob violence in Chauri Chaura in Uttar
Pradesh the previous day, in which provoked Indians burned a
police station, killing 21 policemen and a young boy. Gandhi calls
off the national *satyagraha* campaign. Other leaders, including
Nehru, are dismayed. For many, Gandhi's controversial decision

subverts the national determination for anti-colonial independence, plays into the hands of the British rulers and sets back the potential for unifying class, caste and religious national resistance for decades, if not permanently.

Gandhi sees this differently. For him national political independence is less important than moral and social regeneration, and true independence is impossible without nonviolent, truthful self-restraint and self-rule. Once again he feels that he miscalculated and that India is not ready for a real Non-Cooperation Campaign of strong, courageous *satyagrahis* who embrace and live *ahimsa*. In addition, Gandhi undergoes a fast of self-purification and penance. Although it seems to many that Gandhi is completely impractical and unrealistic in taking personal responsibility for the actions of distant strangers, he operates from a different frame of reference. Tapping into some traditional Indian spiritual positions, as he does repeatedly in later decades, Gandhi believes that an exemplary personal mode of living has efficacious moral and spiritual power. If others act in ways that are untruthful, violent and evil, this is a reflection of his own imperfection. This means that he must do penance for their sins and this requires his greater moral and spiritual development.

On 10 March 1922 police arrest Gandhi at his ashram on grounds of sedition for articles he published in *Young India*. In a remarkable trial on 18 March in Ahmedabad, Gandhi defends himself, but it is really British colonialism that is put on trial. He admits to the legal charge but turns the trial into an indictment of unjust British rule, claiming that it is 'a virtue to be disaffected towards a Government which in its totality has done more harm to India than any previous system'. If the judge agrees with the system, he should inflict the 'severest penalty' to which Gandhi will 'cheerfully submit'. But if the judge disapproves of the prevailing system, it is his duty to condemn the system and then resign. Justice Robert S. Broomfield, moved by Gandhi and his commitment to nonviolence, responds that he is reluctant but required by law to sentence Gandhi. He sentences Gandhi to six years in prison and then states that no one will be more pleased than he if this is later reduced and Gandhi released. The British have learned a lesson. For all of his later arrests and imprisonments, this is the first and only time that Gandhi is allowed to defend himself at a trial.

Discouraged and depressed over the failure of noncooperation and political *satyagraha*, Gandhi turns inward. He devotes most of his time from 1922 to 1928 to nonviolent experiments with truth involving self-rule, personal and social transformation, and different aspects of his Constructive Programme for moral regeneration. He spends two years in prison, often in solitary confinement. His health deteriorates, and after being rushed to hospital for a dangerous appendectomy operation he is released from prison in 1924 on grounds of health. While in prison he has time for meditative self-reflection. He reads the Indian epics, the *Mahabharata* and *Ramayana*, Hindu *Upanishads*, other religious texts and rereads the *Gita*. He develops his analysis of the unity of all existence, including the unity of all religions, and the nature of nonviolence, love, renunciation, selfless service, truth, God, self and reality. In later years Gandhi often describes imprisonment as peaceful and joyful. It is a welcome relief from the overwhelming daily demands of public life and it provides him with time for reading, writing and self-purification.

During his Constructive Programme emphasis in the 1920s, Gandhi focuses on four major concerns which dominate the rest of his life: Hindu–Muslim harmonious relations, the spinning-wheel and decentralized *khadi* production, the removal of untouchability and the social uplift of women. These are not isolated concerns and all address issues of poverty, divisiveness and violence and aim at realizing the fundamental interconnectedness and unity of all existence. Each of these concerns is realized in diverse, complex, difficult, changing, contextual situations, is given many significant reformulations by Gandhi, and raises ongoing controversies and debates about Gandhi and his legacy.[2]

Gandhi, who experienced positive Muslim–Hindu unity in South Africa, places this at the top of his Constructive Programme agenda, but his attempts at unity in India are increasingly failures. In 1919 he is approached by Indian Muslims asking him to support and provide leadership to the postwar Khilafat (Caliphate) movement that attempts to restore the Turkish Sultan to the position of authority held during the Ottoman Empire. Although the Khilafat would seem at odds with Gandhi's views of religion, politics and religious-political relations, he agrees on the condition that the Ali brothers Muhammad and Shaukat and other Khilafat leaders accept nonviolence. For Gandhi, this is a way of supporting Indian Muslims and furthering Hindu–Muslim unity as part of India's struggle for *swaraj*. This is the period of greatest trust and most harmonious Muslim–Hindu relations, but Gandhi's endorsement of Khilafat is baffling and controversial, not just to Hindus but even to most modern Muslim leaders. Even Khilafat Muslims never endorse Gandhi's *ahimsa* as a philosophy, and Hindu–Muslim disunity surfaces in the coming years. Although Gandhi continues to give Hindu–Muslim unity and harmonious relations a high priority throughout the 1930s and 1940s, with rare dramatic exceptions this is a period of deteriorating trust, greater factionalism and increasing multidimensional violence.[3]

Over the decades Gandhi has more success in popularizing the *charka* (spinning-wheel) and *khadi* (handspun cloth), even among many modern Indians who find it a backward technology and premodern economy. After becoming President of the Indian National Congress in 1924, the only time he held such political office, Gandhi founds the non-Congress All-India Spinners' Association in 1925. He becomes increasingly fond of the spinning-wheel and sometimes asserts that it is the indispensable means

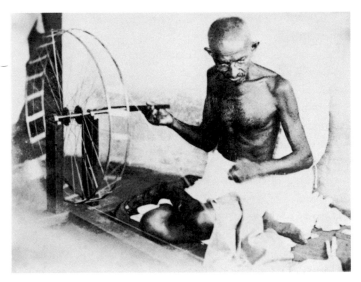

At the spinning-wheel at Sabarmati Ashram, 1925.

to *swaraj*. For Gandhi it functions on many interrelated levels, including symbolically. For India's 700,000 villages and its devastating poverty, emphasizing the spinning-wheel can provide employment, resist the modern 'machine craze' that displaces and dehumanizes labour, and allow for small-scale, decentralized, sustainable economies upholding the dignity of labour. It serves an egalitarian function, allowing the privileged to identify with the plight of the least fortunate and to overcome class, caste and other oppressive relations. It is meditative, as well as productive, integrating mind and body, and provides selfless service to meet the needs of others. It serves as a powerful symbol and means towards the self-reliance and independence of *swaraj, the self-sufficient economy of swadeshi*, the moral economic philosophy of striving for 'the welfare of all' or *sarvodaya*, realizing the Constructive Programme and engaging in nonviolent, unifying *sarvodaya* campaigns.

Recognizing the symbolic is imperative for Gandhi and for interpreting his exemplary model, lessons and legacy, including 'Mahatma Gandhi' as symbol. Gandhi is always very conscious of the need to utilize powerful symbols that not only symbolize specific contextualized issues, injustices and ideals but, even more importantly, are living symbols that key into and activate the deepest forces of nonviolence, truth, love and compassion within us. In this regard, it is commonplace for critics and even some admirers of the historical Gandhi to assert that, say, emphasizing the spinning-wheel and the production of homespun cloth is outdated, impractical and completely irrelevant when addressing issues of the modern globalized economy. However, the issues, concerns and alternative values and approaches symbolically represented by the spinning-wheel are still relevant and significant today.

Removal of untouchability is one of Gandhi's major priorities in the Constructive Programme. For him, if Hinduism cannot remove the blot of untouchability it should cease to exist. In 1924 he supports the Vykom (Vaikom) Satyagraha in Travancore, now part of Kerala, agitating against caste restrictions denying untouch-ables access to public roads near the Shiva Temple. While Gandhi places even greater emphasis on defying traditional regulations and eliminating untouchability during his remaining years in India, this becomes and still is a source of great conflict and controversy. Gandhi, not unexpectedly, is opposed mainly by traditional caste-based Hindus, but also later by various *dalits*, especially followers of Dr B. R. Ambedkar, who – born an untouchable – became an influential jurist, scholar and social reformer. *Dalits* (those who have been 'ground down' or 'broken to pieces') often submit that Gandhi is paternalistic in claiming to speak for untouchables and that he really endorses a reactionary caste system.

Regardless of differing interpretations and positions on these *dalit* issues, it seems clear that Gandhi is always sincere in his opposition to specific institutions and practices of untouchability. Indeed, he is willing to put his family, his ashrams and his life at risk and even to die for this cause. In terms of the larger issues surrounding Gandhi's changing formulations about caste, there is room for debate. However, if one examines Gandhi's personality, his philosophy, his practices, how he actually lives his life, the most adequate interpretation is that Gandhi is at odds with hierarchical, institutionalized, caste-based Hinduism and that Gandhi's message is essentially anti-caste.

Finally, the social uplift of women becomes a major pillar in Gandhi's Constructive Programme in the 1920s and for the rest of his life. Starting as the abusive, domineering, patriarchal Mohandas, Gandhi radically transforms and remakes himself in his approach to women and gender relations. What is most significant in his ashram work, as well as in his approach to gender relations in society at large, is his radical egalitarianism, with his strong critique of male domination and his affirmation that women should be treated with respect as equal human beings entitled to equal freedom and opportunities. His evolved position is that gender relations should be morally and spiritually constituted by equal partners. At times Gandhi even claims that women are superior since they most express his values of nonviolence, love, patience, empathy, voluntary suffering and selfless service.

Such egalitarian and lofty views of women do not remove all controversies, including some of Gandhi's limited and reactionary views on gender. This is evidenced in some of his male-language normative formulations and in his reactionary formulations on birth control measures as unnatural and immoral, and his disturbing passages on the personal responsibility and recommended responses of rape victims. Gandhi's inadequate approach is evident in his reactionary views of the undesirability of sexual relations except for reproduction, and his dismissal of any positive value to sexual pleasure, as well as his scandalous experiments with *brahmacharya* late in life (see chapter Five).

What is truly astounding in the Constructive Programme and the freedom struggle is how millions of Indian women are so attracted to Gandhi and his message. He often appears to them as embodying 'the feminine' and as more androgynous than exclusively male. In their dominant contexts of repressive male-dominated violence they are drawn to Gandhi and his more secure and comforting message of nonviolence. As is the case with millions of illiterate peasants, male and female, women often feel that Gandhi really understands and identifies with their difficult situations and that he is willing to sacrifice everything for their social uplift. Remarkably, they courageously defy family, caste, religious and other social taboos and coercive measures and become active participants in the Constructive Programme and the *satya-graha* struggles. In general Gandhi's Constructive Programme regarding women and gender equality is far ahead of its time in India of the 1920s and, in its basic egalitarian relational values, remains ahead of its time in contemporary India and the world.

Gandhi returns to active public political life in 1928, after the British government establishes a constitutional reform commission under Sir John Simon that includes no Indian members. In the anti-Simon Commission atmosphere, Congress considers the Nehru Report, named after Motilal Nehru, Jawaharlal's father, which calls for Dominion Status for India. At the December Congress Party meeting in Calcutta, Gandhi pushes through a resolution giving the British government one year to grant India dominion status or face a new campaign of noncooperation with the goal of complete independence. As is often the case, Gandhi shows great skill in mediating conflicting positions in the Indian National Congress and arriving at a compromise. He moderates the more forceful views of the younger Jawaharlal Nehru, Subhas Chandra Bose and others who demand immediate complete independence, and he pushes others beyond the self-imposed limits of their gradual legal appeals for modest reform. When the British do not respond, the Indian flag is unfurled at the Lahore Congress session on 31 December. *Swaraj* is to mean *Purna Swaraj* or complete independence and 26 January 1930 is to be celebrated as India's Independence Day. In post-colonial India 15 August, the date selected by the British for India's independence in 1947, is celebrated as Independence Day, and 26 January, the date selected by Congress, remains a major national holiday celebrated as India's Republic Day.

Gandhi's previously shattered faith in nonviolent political struggle is renewed after the economic Bardoli Satyagraha of 1928, under the leadership of Sardar Patel, in which rural Gujarati peasants are victorious in defying the greatly increased land revenue assessments and higher taxes. Consistent with the Calcutta Congress resolution, Gandhi is authorized by Congress to head up a new campaign of nonviolent noncooperation and civil disobedience.

In February 1930 Gandhi decides to organize the *satyagraha* against the British tax on salt. His choice of salt, as opposed to complete independence or some other lofty goal, baffles not only the British rulers but also his Congress supporters. Once again, others misunderstand and underestimate Gandhi's contextual insights, capacity to identify with and motivate the Indian masses and brilliant use of powerful symbols to reveal injustices and activate nonviolent forces for moral regeneration.

Gandhi launches the Salt March from his Sabarmati Ashram on 12 March, not initially as a mass *satyagraha* but as Gandhi's *satyagraha*, consisting of 78 carefully chosen ashram *satyagrahis*, who undertake the 241-mile march to the seacoast village of Dandi. Gandhi spends time each day during the 24-day march citing religious scriptures, opposing poverty and alcoholism and child-marriages, promoting other principles of constructive work, as

Gandhi leads the Salt March, his most famous nonviolent civil disobedience action, 12 March 1930.

well as advocating nonviolent civil disobedience of the salt tax. Participation and excitement grow, as Gandhi skilfully manages local, national and international coverage. For Gandhi and millions of others, nonviolence and truth are on the march. Arriving at Dandi on 5 April, Gandhi goes to the sea coast the next morning and picks up the natural salt, thus defying the government's ban. Gandhi's example spreads like a 'prairie fire', in Nehru's admiring words, and millions become involved in manufacturing, selling and buying illegal salt. Many are beaten and over 60,000, including Gandhi, arrested.

The Salt Satyagraha and its aftermath reveal Gandhi at his most impressive moral and spiritual way of being in the world.[4] He upholds truth and nonviolence through Constructive Programme and action-oriented *satyagraha*. As with the spinning-wheel, salt has immediate, visible, practical dimensions, but it has even greater symbolic dimensions going far beyond the issue of the specific salt tax. On the most basic level of need salt is a necessity of life, and Indians, especially the impoverished masses, are denied access and unfairly burdened. Salt Satyagraha is a way that the privileged can identify with and relate selflessly and compassionately to the needs of the untouchables and others who are most impoverished, exploited and oppressed. Salt Satyagraha, focusing on a universal need, can unite Muslims and Hindus, the religious and nonreligious, different classes and castes, men and women. In fact many observe that this campaign is remarkable for the widespread participation of women, who experience resistance to salt tax injustice as integrating the personal in their lives with the political.

In larger terms the Salt Satyagraha goes far beyond salt and dramatically symbolizes and brings into clear daylight not only the injustices and violence of British colonial domination but also the basic human right to have access to necessities to meet human needs, the basic human duty or *dharma* to provide for those rights, the basic equality and integrity and unity of all human beings and the need to motivate and activate our nonviolent truth-force and love-force through noncooperation with evil and injustice.

The Salt Satyagraha represents the high point of Gandhi's nonviolent campaigns and the time of his greatest influence. It is his best organized, most disciplined and most effective nonviolent campaign in exposing the injustice, moral bankruptcy and violence of British rule in India and the moral superiority of the nonviolent Indian struggle for freedom and independence. The period of the Salt March and civil disobedience, extending through Gandhi's participation as the sole representative of the Indian National Congress at the Round Table Conference in London in 1931, is the high point in Gandhi's popularity and prestige. He appears to hundreds of millions not only as the fearless, self-sacrificing Indian national leader, but also emerges as a greatly admired international figure of exemplary moral and spiritual virtue. As said at the time, the Salt Satyagraha marks the end of British colonial rule and the independence of India, even if it takes an additional seventeen difficult years to achieve.

4

From the Round Table
to 'Constructive Work'

A month after his salt civil disobedience Gandhi comes up with
the idea of raiding the government salt depot in Dharasana, 25
miles from Dandi. Before that can take place he is arrested and
taken to the Yeravda jail in Poona (Pune), and his sixth imprisonment lasts from 5 May 1930 to 26 January 1931. On 21 May, under
the leadership of Sarojini Naidu (freedom fighter, poet and close
Gandhi associate) and others, and as vividly reported by American
correspondent Webb Miller and portrayed in the movie *Gandhi*,
hundreds of disciplined nonviolent *satyagrahis* are savagely beaten.
Other forms of nonviolent resistance spread throughout India
against importing foreign cloth and paying land revenues. Many
village officials submit their resignations as part of the resistance.
At the instructions of Lord Irwin (Viceroy, April 1926 to April
1931) Gandhi is released from jail and the two participate in
a series of meetings. This results in the Irwin–Gandhi Pact by
which thousands of prisoners are released, and Gandhi terminates
the civil disobedience. The Pact does not grant India Dominion
Status or Independence. Instead, Irwin invites Gandhi to come to
London for the Second Round Table Conference to discuss India's
future status.

Gandhi's fascinating visit to England is widely publicized.
Well known are the images of Gandhi in a loincloth meeting with
King George v at Buckingham Palace and later being contemp-
tuously dismissed by Churchill as the 'half-naked fakir'. When

asked about being so underdressed, Gandhi, with typical humour, responds that 'the King had enough on for both of us'. Asked about Churchill's condemnation, Gandhi responds that he takes this as a 'compliment', but he is far too modest and unworthy to be a half-naked fakir. Also well known are the images of Gandhi happily interacting with the poor of London's East End and with Lancashire cotton weavers.

As sole Congress Party representative, Gandhi, always uncomfortable with such formal political negotiations and without flexibility and authority to negotiate for all of India, has limited expectations. Nevertheless, he and other Indians are dismayed by how the British conduct the conference and are disappointed with the absence of any productive results. Using their typical colonial divide-and-rule approach, the British emphasize their responsibility to protect the rights of India's minorities. In this way they disempower the potential for a unified, anti-colonial, Indian nationalist presence. They limit Gandhi's voice and authority

Mahatma Gandhi, with Madan Mohan Malaviya (far left), Sarojini Naidu, one of his most dedicated associates (to his right), and Kasturba Gandhi, about to embark at Mumbai (Bombay) on the SS *Rajputana* for England, 29 August 1931.

With women textiles workers at Lancashire, England, 26 September 1931.

by inviting the participation of Muslim, untouchable and princely
state representatives who have their own conflicting interests and
agendas. Most troubling to Gandhi is the promotion of untouchables as a separate electorate, similar to the separate Muslim
electorate, or separate Sikh and European electorates, and not
as an integral part of majority Hindu society.

Indian leaders, both within and outside the Congress Party,
use Gandhi's failure to achieve results to raise doubts about the
effectiveness of his approach. They promote non-Gandhi and
anti-Gandhi anti-colonial approaches and goals. This pattern of
contested alternative leadership and approaches continues to grow
during the 1930s and 1940s and in many ways Gandhi's authority,
control and influence have peaked and will now gradually decline.

Far more interesting and enjoyable for Gandhi is what he
does outside the conference. He is most at home living at Muriel
Lester's Kingsley Hall in the slums of London and interacting with
the English working-class poor, including children. In a difficult

At the Second Round Table Conference in London, November 1931.

situation he is persuasive and able to win over the goodwill and support of mill workers, who have encountered extreme hardships exacerbated by Gandhi's *swadeshi* boycott of foreign cloth. Gandhi has enjoyable meetings with George Bernard Shaw, Charlie Chaplin and other noted personalities. He has several rewarding experiences on the return trip. These include conversations in Geneva with the novelist and pacifist Romain Rolland, who had written a book about Gandhi in 1924 and made him known in Europe.[1] Gandhi also visits the Sistine Chapel at the Vatican, where he is impressed by a crucifix by the altar, a symbol of voluntary suffering and self-sacrifice that he often cites as expressing his philosophy of truth and nonviolence.

Gandhi returns to Bombay on 28 December, two days after Nehru is arrested, and he finds a very different, much more repressive environment. On 4 January he is arrested at Mani Bhavan in Bombay and imprisoned at Yeravda jail. Lord Willingdon, who

Gandhi, Maraben (centre) and Pandit Madan Mohan Malaviya (right) inspecting goats at the Dairy Show at the Royal Agricultural Hall, Islington, London, 23 October 1931. The prize-winning goat was named 'Mahatma Gandhi'.

serves as Viceroy from April 1931 to April 1936, has no desire to negotiate with Gandhi and is determined to crush Indian anti-colonial resistance.

Gandhi now rededicates himself to eliminating the blot of untouchability. The traditional hierarchical Hindu caste system codification assigns the 'untouchables' or 'outcastes', also classified as belonging to the 'Depressed' or 'Suppressed' Classes, to the bottom rung, doing the most menial and karmically polluting tasks. From 1932 Gandhi uses the term *Harijans* ('children of God' or 'people of God') instead of 'untouchables' and in February 1933, he launches his weekly, *Harijan*. Some untouchables, especially those identified with Bhimrao R. Ambedkar, find Gandhi's term paternalistic, and they prefer *Dalits* ('the broken' and 'oppressed'), a term used by many scholars and activists today.[2]

Gandhi's greatest fear from the Round Table conference proves true, and in the Communal Award of 17 August 1932 the British grant the separate electorate for 'untouchables'. Ambedkar, who strongly condemns the caste system and distrusts hierarchical Hinduism, favours this kind of 'identity politics' in which *Dalits* can represent themselves. Gandhi, who is more careful in his criticism of the Vedic authoritarian scriptures and caste Hinduism, strongly opposes the separate electorate. For him *Harijans* are equal integral members of Hindu society, and unless Hinduism can radically reform itself and abolish untouchability it has no right to exist. Consistent with his inclusive philosophy of privileging the needs of the least fortunate, Gandhi favours a greater number of 'reserved seats' for untouchables for which all Hindus can vote.

On 20 September 1932 Gandhi begins a fast unto death unless the British revoke the special electorate for untouchables. Ambedkar regards this as a 'political stunt', coercively forcing him to choose between saving the Mahatma's life or the rights of his people. Gandhi sees his fast as noncoercive. He hopes to 'sting the Hindu conscience' into right action, but he must do what his conscience instructs him to do, even if it results in his death. After hard bargaining, Gandhi and Ambedkar, along with leaders of caste Hindus and untouchables, agree to the Poona Pact. In this compromise the untouchables are not classified as a separate electorate but they are to receive 148 reserved legislative seats instead of the 78 previously granted under the British award. No Hindu will be treated as an untouchable, caste Hindus will remove restrictions and the demeaning ways they have oppressed *Harijans*, and there will be greater support for the education of untouchables. Gandhi breaks his fast on 25 September.

In late April 1933 Gandhi announces his intention to undergo an anti-untouchability 21-day fast. On 8 May, after considerable publicity and concern by others, he commences his fast. He is released from prison later that day. With renewed dedication

Gandhi focuses on untouchability. From Wardha, on 7 November 1933, he launches his all-India tour for the uplift of *Harijans*. The tour includes speeches, fundraising and the entry of temples and wells, and ends in Banaras on 29 July 1934.

This begins a period, lasting until the early 1940s, when Gandhi, as he did in the 1920s, tends to withdraw from public political life, although not always successfully. He now focuses on village work and the Constructive Programme with an emphasis on education, eradicating untouchability, establishing Hindu–Muslim and gender and other harmonious relations, and working in other ways to create models for exemplary moral and spiritual village life.

On 27 October 1934 Gandhi inaugurates the All-India Village Industries Association and several days later, at the session of the Congress held in Bombay under the presidency of Rajendra Prasad, later the first president of independent India, Gandhi formally resigns from the Indian National Congress. Although he is still revered and the Congress leadership reluctantly accepts his resignation, Gandhi feels that there are growing significant differences between his priorities and those of the other leaders, and that they should now be free to lead Congress and the independence movements in ways they deem best.

Gandhi moves to Wardha in central India and in 1936 establishes the Sevagram Ashram five miles away in a very undeveloped village. For Gandhi, this allows him to greatly simplify his life and to engage in experiments with truth in creating an exemplary model of village living for India's future. After many decades of experiments with truth involving the theory and practice of 'constructive work', Gandhi formulates the fundamental features of his programme for *poorna swaraj*, or complete independence. As formulated in Gandhi's *Constructive Programme: Its Meaning and Place*, published in 1941, these experiments in uplifting village life are grounded in his philosophy and practices of truth and nonviolence and selfless service to meet the needs of others. This is Gandhi's outline of a programme for unifying the haves and have-nots, radically transforming human relations, overcoming the violent and unjust structures of domination and allowing individuals and society to develop in ways that express everyone's highest moral and spiritual potentialities.[3]

In his *Constructive Programme* Gandhi begins with communal and religious unity. Other priorities include the removal of untouchability, the prohibition of alcohol and other intoxicants, the development of *khadi* and other village industries, village sanitation and education in health and hygiene. He promotes New or Basic Education and adult education, the uplift of women, the focus on provincial languages and making Hindi (or Hindi–Urdu) the national language. Additional priorities include the uplift of peasants and other workers and economic equality, the uplift of *adivasi*s ('original peoples', 'indigenous peoples', tribals), meeting the needs of lepers, granting an important role for students and recognizing the very limited use of civil disobedience.

A major aspect of Gandhi's constructive work in his 'whole village work' focuses on economic relations that are nonviolent, truthful, decentralized and egalitarian. They involve self-restraint and the simplification of needs, emphasize economic self-sufficient independence (*swadeshi*), allow the individual to develop toward greater self-reliance and freedom (*swaraj*) and further the economic philosophy of the welfare of all (*sarvodaya*). For Gandhi such economic relations are sustainable, provide for the harmonious integration of body, mind and heart or soul, and are grounded in virtuous selfless service. This moral economy is often identified as 'Gandhian socialism' with its essential commitment to truth and nonviolence. Gandhi is very critical of 'modern' economics with its profit and money-oriented 'machine craze' and exploitation of labour. He emphasizes the spinning-wheel, *khadi*, simple human-centric labour-intensive work with limited use of technology, and crafts and vocational work as most appropriate for the contextual conditions and needs of India's villages, which, for Gandhi, is usually seen as 'the real India'.[4]

Much of this is controversial during Gandhi's life and is rejected by Nehru and others as anti-modern and no model for India's future. It is even more controversial today as those with economic power in India and in the world find such an anti-modern economy backward and irrelevant for dealing with contexts of present technology, corporate and financial capitalism and globalization. Gandhi's economic programme seems hopelessly irrelevant if one takes it literally, applies it rigidly and then focuses on *khadi*, the spinning-wheel and the primacy of vocational and craft production instead of focusing on the basic moral and spiritual priorities and regulative ideals underlying Gandhi's economic philosophy and practices.

In this regard, Gandhi repeatedly tells us that he is not against the machine or technology if it enables greater human development and liberation. But he is against the modern worship of the machine that marginalizes real human needs and concerns, displaces humans when there is a surplus of labour that needs to be employed, and expresses technological relations that involve inequality, objectification, alienation and domination. When one examines Gandhi's basic economic priorities in a selective and reformulated way – his emphasis on decentralized more egalitarian democratic relations that empower the individual and the community, on relations that reflect human dignity, integrity and well-being, and on alternative technologies and relations that are economically, socially and environmentally sustainable – then much of his economic constructive work may be very relevant to our contemporary contexts.

A related significant aspect of Gandhi's village constructive work focuses on a radically different model of education. In October 1937 he inaugurates the New Education Conference at Wardha, where he formulates his *Nai Talim* ('New Education'). As a moral and spiritual visionary, who considers himself a pragmatic idealist,

Gandhi focuses on educational transformative practices. Educate students and others in specific ways, based on proper values, and this will lead to individuals and social groupings that are moral, express character and virtue, are nonviolent and loving and truthful, and avoid the violence and untruthfulness of educational approaches that are part of 'modern civilization'.[5]

For Gandhi, modern Western education, as evidenced in the education of privileged Indians under the Raj, is violent, untruthful, immoral, egotistical and adversarial. It miseducates students to 'succeed' in economic, political, social, cultural and civilizational relations of domination, injustice, oppression and exploitation. By way of extreme contrast, Gandhi's approach to education emphasizes character and moral development, rather than 'book learning' and 'formal education'. Truly educated students have exemplary moral character, express the 'higher' human forces of love and nonviolence, are fearless and courageous and in all ways virtuous. They have let go of ego needs for wealth and power, and are motivated to fulfil their *dharma* of social and moral duty through selfless service. Responding to the contextual conditions and needs of village India, Gandhi proposes decentralized village education free of state support and controls, using local or regional languages instead of English, giving priorities to crafts and vocational education with the development of small-scale village industries and emphasizing the harmonious development of mind, body and heart or spirit in each student through the integration of knowledge and work.

As with his Constructive Programme of economics, Gandhi's philosophy and practices of education were controversial during his lifetime and are even more controversial today. The failure of Gandhi's educational vision and practices may be illustrated by what happens in the ashram education of his children, especially the tragic life of his oldest son, Harilal. Although there are other determining factors, it is significant that Gandhi repeatedly denies his oldest son his desire for a modern education, including Harilal's desire to follow in his father's footsteps and become a lawyer. Harilal's rigidly controlled education and socialization contribute to his development as a resentful, angry, conflicted person, never at peace with himself and estranged from his father, with many addictions, including alcoholism and wasteful financial expenditure. His troubled life includes a temporary, highly publicized conversion to Islam, and ends with a sad death, several months after Gandhi's assassination, in the most impoverished conditions of degeneration.[6]

Taken literally and applied rigidly, Gandhi's pronouncements on education, with his focus on vocational training and village crafts, often seem hopelessly reactionary and irrelevant. It is easy to conclude that Gandhi's educational constructive work is out of date and completely irrelevant for the needs and priorities of today's world, including a modern Indian education that focuses on the most advanced scientific, technological, engineering, medical, business, media, state and military developments.

Once again, the insights and relevance of Gandhi's Constructive Programme of education depend on not only discarding what is hopelessly reactionary and irrelevant to present contexts, but also on focusing on and reinterpreting Gandhi's basic ethical and spiritual priorities. One of Gandhi's famous 'Seven Social Sins' is 'knowledge without character', sometimes presented as 'education without character'.[7] Educators today are increasingly disturbed by the fact that they are turning out students with scientific, technological, business and other skills, who can often gain money and power, but who lack character or any worthy human values and commitments. As Gandhi repeatedly warns, such power without character and values is very dangerous and leads to conflict, violence, suffering and an unhappy and unsustainable way of life.

In this regard Gandhi's basic education focuses on taking each individual student as a unique valuable person, with the need to develop harmonious relations of mind, body and heart. Truly educated students are those who know how to live worthy moral and truthful lives with character, virtues and nonegoistic service. They live lives of empathy, compassion, love, self-restraint and a willingness to sacrifice and suffer without sacrificing others and inflicting suffering on them. Such an approach to education may be not only relevant but also urgently needed to meet our educational crises, which are part of our human civilizational crises.

As noted, Gandhi addresses the first section of his published *Constructive Programme* to communal and religious unity and harmony. In terms of family upbringing, experiences in England and South Africa and other formative influences, Gandhi gives this topic one of his highest priorities in India. He develops a dynamic, contextualized, complex and nuanced theory and practice of religion and culture, of interreligious and intercultural dialogue and relations, that often place him at odds with those who uphold conservative traditional religious and cultural authority. Gandhi maintains that no religion or culture has the absolute truth, that all scriptures and other foundational texts are transmitted through and constructed by imperfect human beings and that, while upholding what is best in our own religion and culture, we can learn from truths that others have experienced. For Gandhi, only such a dynamic and open-ended developmental approach of humility, empathy, tolerance and mutual respect can deal with the root causes and major causal determinants of so much religious and cultural misunderstanding, intolerance, disunity, disharmony, conflict, violence and war.

In this regard Gandhi's major focus is on Hindu–Muslim unity and harmonious relations. This is an earlier priority in his life and the so-called 'Muslim question' and Muslim–Hindu relations now consume much of Gandhi's time for the remainder of the 1930s and until his assassination in January 1948. There are certainly many encouraging and mixed experiences and Gandhi continues to enjoy the deep respect of and close friendship with many influential Muslim leaders. These include Abdul Kalam Azad, popularly known as Maulana Azad, who is elected as Indian National Congress President in 1923 and 1940 and is India's first Minister of Education, and the remarkable Pashtun leader of nonviolent resistance and follower of Mahatma Gandhi, Abdul Ghaffar Khan (or Badshah Khan), known as the 'frontier Gandhi'. Nevertheless, at least from the late 1930s Muslim–Hindu relations keep deteriorating, and Gandhi winds up at the time of Partition, with the overwhelming violence and suffering of communal riots and savage killings, in a state of deep despair, feeling that no one listens to him and that he is a failure.

Much of this deterioration in communal religious relations can be traced back to Britain's Government of India Act of 1935 that greatly enlarges the Indian electorate and establishes a provincial political system that has considerable freedom. In the subsequent provincial elections of 1937 the Indian National Congress gains significant political power by winning in seven of the eleven provinces. However, it does not poll well among Indian Muslims, although the Indian Muslim League under the leadership of Muhammad Ali Jinnah does not enjoy great support from the Muslim population either. During 1937–9 Congress attempts to win over Indian Muslims but Jinnah and the Muslim League effectively counter this by arousing Muslims' fears and insecurities and moving Muslims in a separate, communal, religious nationalist direction.

Gandhi's failure in achieving Hindu–Muslim unity and harmony is usually analysed in terms of his 'adversary' M. A. Jinnah's personality and approach and their strained relations. Jinnah has a very complex and often contradictory personality and orientation. In many respects he has more in common with Gandhi than does Subhas Chandra Bose and many other Hindu Congress leaders. Jinnah and Gandhi come from the same part of India, speak the same Gujarati language, are trained as lawyers in London and are leaders in the Indian National Congress working for Muslim–Hindu unity in one independent India.

Ironically, considering his later determined commitment to a separate Islamic religious nation of Pakistan, Jinnah is a very modern, nonreligious Indian, enjoying expensive Western clothes, alcohol and even pork. Jinnah is what Gandhi classifies under 'the moderates': elite, privileged, highly educated, Westernized, 'modern' Indians who negotiate with the British for formal, legal, constitutional reforms. Jinnah is always uncomfortable and distrustful of Gandhi, his philosophy and his practices. Gandhi seems repeatedly to critique, subvert and mobilize against what Jinnah proposes and takes to be rational, modern and progressive. Jinnah distrusts Gandhi's charming personality and charisma and how he can use his authority to mobilize the forces of millions of illiterate, premodern, 'backward' peasants.

Although Gandhi reaches out repeatedly to Jinnah and Indian Muslims, relations with Jinnah, Congress–Muslim League relations and Hindu–Muslim relations keep deteriorating. Scholars present many reasons for the escalating tensions and antagonistic contradictions that result in so much violence and suffering and that continue to the present. There is certainly considerable evidence to present Jinnah as the villain, an unattractive, stubborn, egotistical, hypocritical opportunist, who exacerbates communal fears and tensions and works against Hindu–Muslim unity. This portrayal is even more vivid when Jinnah is contrasted with the moral and spiritual Gandhi, who is willing to sacrifice his life for Hindu–Muslim harmony. However, contextual conditions and alternatives are much more complex than this simple portrayal.

The most fundamental cause for the deteriorating Hindu–Muslim relations involves the basic difference between Gandhi and Jinnah, and his Muslim League, in how they finally view the status of Indian Muslims and the future of a Hindu-majority India.

Jinnah and the Muslim League develop a communal view that Muslims and Hindus are two separate 'nations'. Gandhi can empathize with other points of view and can offer concessions and compromises but he can never accept this 'two-nation' theory. For Gandhi, with his commitment to communal and religious unity and harmony, Muslims and Hindus may have different paths to the truth, but in terms of their shared history, culture, language and underlying ethical and spiritual truths, they are part of one glorious Indian civilization. Without Gandhi's essential commitment to interreligious and intercultural unity and harmony Jinnah and the Muslim League reject his philosophy and his proposals. They increasingly develop the view that a unified India will be a Hindu 'nation', under the rule of a tyranny of the majority, who will subject the separate minority Muslim 'nation' to discrimination, second-class citizenship, violation of what is required for their separate religious identity and possible reprisals as a reaction to India's history of violent Muslim invasions and rule.

It is open to debate to what extent Gandhi is responsible for this failure. Does he make serious errors and miscalculations in his formulations and approaches to different Muslim leaders? To what extent do the real contextual forces, leading personalities and historical conditions, including the outbreak of the Second World War and British colonial policies, prevent a well-intentioned Gandhi from being able to control Hindu–Muslim relations? What is clear is that he is largely unsuccessful in this important aim of his constructive work.

Looking back to the 1930s, with Gandhi's major focus on his Constructive Programme, it is evident that his constructive work has some impressive but often mixed results. This assessment includes the importance he places on his new headquarters in developing his model ashram at Sevagram. Unlike many other leaders, who withdraw from society and establish small, alternative communities of followers, Gandhi is a moral and spiritual pragmatist, who wants his constructive work at the ashram to serve as an exemplary moral transformative model. He is engaged in constructive work experiments with truth with the aim of radically changing the dominant economic, social and cultural priorities and relations of village life, of India and even of the world.

Gandhi walking at Sevagram Ashram, 1945.

Even in evaluating Sevagram, Gandhi regretfully reflects that seemingly committed followers are often primarily motivated by their desire to be in the presence of the Mahatma, and never accept the philosophy of the Constructive Programme as a total way of life. And since he remains the most revered national leader, with frequent demands from Congress and others, Gandhi cannot devote the time and effort necessary for dealing with the conflicts and tensions around the formulation and implementation of the Constructive Programme.

Gandhi's rueful reflections are similar to those about the lack of true commitment to *ahimsa* and *satyagraha*, as seen in the early 1920s and especially late in his life. He realizes that his millions of followers, even many of the more dedicated ashramites and *satyagrahis*, only seem to accept *ahimsa*, *satyagraha* and the Constructive Programme. They really accept these because of their admiration for Bapu, their Father, the exalted Mahatma, and on tactical and strategic grounds, as practical options that can work. However, most never accept nonviolence, truth-force and constructive work as creeds, philosophies and committed total ways of life. That is why, under different contextual situations, they change their priorities and tactics and violate the basic values and teachings of these philosophies. And that is why Gandhi and India repeatedly experience so much violence, hatred, untruthfulness, replication of the evils of modern civilization and religious and communal disharmony.

As Gandhi often expresses it, in our common non-Gandhian tactical approach we experience 'nonviolence' that is really multi-dimensional and structural violence, 'peace' that really expresses a state of war, 'truth' that is deeply untruthful, professions of love and unity and harmony that are always short lived and often turn into their opposites. For example, as Gandhi sadly reflects, what we usually call the nonviolent resistance of '*satyagraha*' lacks the moral and spiritual development of courage, fearlessness and selfless sacrifice. It is therefore a false '*satyagraha* of the weak', and not the true '*satyagraha* of the strong'. Without the creed and philosophy of the morally and spiritually strong, of those who are virtuous and courageous, are willing to suffer and sacrifice and to act according to their duty of nonegoistic selfless service, the transformative efforts to realize truth and nonviolence through *satyagraha* and the Constructive Programme will be temporary, limited and full of failures.

5

From 'Quit India' to Gandhi's Assassination

On 1 September 1939 Nazi Germany invades Poland. Two days later France and Britain declare war on Germany. Lord Linlithgow, British Viceroy from April 1936 to October 1943, announces India's entry into the war without consulting any of the Congress leaders, who are understandably offended. During the war more than 2.5 million Indian troops fight on the side of the Allies.

Indian reactions to the British war effort are mixed. On the one hand, Gandhi, Azad, Patel and other Congress leaders are very opposed to German fascism, and Gandhi initially favours 'nonviolent moral support' for the British. On the other hand, as Nehru and others point out, there's a basic hypocrisy between enlisting Indians in the struggle for freedom from Nazi aggression, while at the same time denying India its basic freedom. Gandhi agrees, and in contrast to his positions in South Africa and in the First World War, he declares that India cannot support the British war effort as long as it is denied its freedom and independence.

British war policies greatly shape the lives of Gandhi, other Indian leaders and the future of India. Britain intensifies its ruthless and repressive polices, with many thousands of Indians killed and arrested, including Gandhi and the other Congress leaders. Relations between the Indian National Congress and the British Raj become increasingly strained and this opens up opportunities for Jinnah and the Muslim League to rapidly increase their influence and power with the British rulers and with the Muslim masses.

Gandhi's position on the British war effort and the need for India's complete independence satisfies neither pro-British nor anti-British Indians. On the one hand, there is widespread opposition in India to fascist aggression and sympathy for helping Britain in its perilous time of need. On the other hand, there is anti-colonial opposition in India that views Gandhi's nonviolent position as insufficient for exploiting Britain's weakness in this time of need.

After attempts at negotiations with the British over steps leading toward independence fail, Congress, at its annual session in March 1940, assigns full authority to Gandhi for conducting a new campaign of civil disobedience. Gandhi, assessing that India is not prepared for national mass *satyagraha*, focuses on individual civil disobedience. He decides on a narrow focus: to defy the British rule prohibiting free speech by promoting the position that one should uphold nonviolent resistance to all war and should not

Nobel Laureate Rabindranath Tagore delivering the address of welcome to Gandhi and his wife Kasturba at Santiniketan (Bengal), 18 February 1940.

help the British war effort. With sole authority and careful control Gandhi rejects most of the volunteers as unqualified to participate as *satyagrahis*. Although many thousands of Indians are arrested during the war, neither this nor later campaigns ever capture the national imagination and loyalty of earlier nonviolent civil disobedience, as in the Salt March Satyagraha. As influenced by larger contextual events, especially German aggression in Europe and Japanese aggression in other parts of Asia, Gandhi's appeals to nonviolence and nonviolent resistance now strike most Indians, even Congress leaders, as rather weak and out of touch with reality.

By 1942 Gandhi realizes that India's campaign for independence must be greatly intensified and he drafts his famous 'Quit India Resolution' for the Congress Working Committee. At the 7 August 1942 gathering in Bombay, after dramatic speeches by Azad, Nehru, Patel and others, Congress representatives overwhelmingly pass the Quit India Resolution. Gandhi speaks for two hours and concludes with his famous dictum for the nonviolent soldier of freedom: 'Do or Die'.

Quit India is India's clearest and most forceful struggle determined to end British rule. Gandhi and other Indian leaders make clear that they will not support the British war effort unless India is granted complete independence. Over 100,000 are immediately arrested and thousands killed or injured. There are many examples of violence on the part of resisting Indians. There is also a significant change in Gandhi's approach. Although he still affirms his total faith in nonviolence, he now lets it be known that this is a 'do or die' Quit India struggle to the end and he will not call off the campaign if individual Indians commit violent acts. Even taking into account that Gandhi no longer enjoys the authority, influence and control that he had in his earlier campaigns, this is one of many significant examples showing how Gandhi is often surprisingly flexible and changes earlier positions in response to new contextual situations.

Two days after the Quit India proclamation Gandhi and the entire Congress Working Committee are arrested in Bombay. Gandhi is imprisoned from 9 August 1942 to 6 May 1944 at the Aga Khan Palace near Poona. Here he experiences two terrible personal blows. On 15 August, after only six days of imprisonment, Gandhi's personal secretary Mahadev Desai dies of a heart attack. For many years Gandhi has depended on Desai as one of his most trusted and closest associates. On 22 February 1944, after eighteen months of imprisonment, Kasturba dies. This shared time of imprisonment is when Gandhi draws closest to his wife. He tries to teach her, greatly appreciates what a strong, admirable, loving companion she has been, realizes how dependent he has been on her and is devastated by her death. Six weeks later, already in a weakened state, Gandhi suffers a bout of malaria and the government, fearing that he will die a martyr in prison, grants his unconditional release on medical grounds.

This period of imprisonment can be viewed in mixed terms. Well into his seventies, with larger developments in India and in the world outside his authority and influence, Gandhi is isolated, plagued by self-doubt and depression, suffers personal loss and is in a state of weakened health. In 1943 he undertakes a 21 day fast, and others, including the government, are fearful that he will die. However, as he had before, Gandhi welcomes imprisonment as a joyful time of voluntary suffering, reading and writing, spinning and constructive work, prayer and self-reflection, personal growth and inner peace. In many ways he emerges from his ordeal ready for the last inspirational years of his life, with a strengthened clarity of purpose. In a period that still astounds his greatest admirers Gandhi now focuses on what must be done, formulates some of his most insightful analysis and discovers an unexpected source of moral energy and rededication in pursuing truth and nonviolence.

After his release and for the rest of his life Gandhi works tirelessly against all odds to restore Hindu–Muslim unity and to avert the division of India into two nations based on irreconcilable religious differences. In September 1944 he visits Jinnah for 18-day talks on Muslim–Hindu unity that prove fruitless. He keeps reaching out to Jinnah and other Muslims, trying to allay their fears of Hindu domination and repression. At one point he desperately proposes that Jinnah be selected as prime minister with the power to appoint his own Muslim Cabinet. By the time of the provincial elections of December 1945 more than 90 per cent of Hindus vote for Congress and more than 90 per cent of Muslims vote for the Muslim League. Gandhi's proposals for religious unity, while inflaming Hindu nationalist anger that he is giving too much away to Muslims, are ignored or dismissed by both Congress and Muslim League as unworkable.

After the war the new Labour Party Government and Lord Wavell, Viceroy from October 1943 to February 1947, realize that India's independence is imminent, and they begin to work for transfer of power. Gandhi is often consulted and has many

With Muslim leader Muhammed Ali Jinnah at Mumbai, September 1944.

Lord Frederick Pethick-Lawrence, Leader of the Cabinet Mission, and Gandhi at Delhi, 18 April 1946.

meetings with Sir Stafford Cripps, Wavell and other British administrators, the British Cabinet Mission discussing transition during 1946, and the last Viceroy Mountbatten (February to August 1947). He continues to interact with Indian leaders in Congress, the Muslim League and others. He agrees to participate as advisor to the Cabinet Mission at the May 1946 Simla Conference at which Congress and the League cannot reach agreement. When the Cabinet Mission proposes a united India with an Interim Government the League calls for a 'Direct Action Day' of protests and this unleashes terrible violence in Calcutta and then elsewhere. Although millions still hold Gandhi in awe as an exemplary moral and spiritual figure and many Indian and British officials still admire him personally, it seems that events have passed him by. No one seems to be listening any more to his advice based on his philosophy of truth and nonviolence.

Two specific issues involve Gandhi controversies and have become the source of debate and major attacks on Gandhi, his philosophy and advocated practices: his advice to Jews facing Nazi genocide and his *brahmacharya* sexual experiments with young Indian women.

Although there are Gandhi defenders, critics and most admirers are disturbed, even appalled, by Gandhi's advice to European Jews facing the Holocaust: that they act like his *satyagrahis* in India, reach out lovingly and nonviolently to Hitler and the Nazis, be willing to sacrifice and suffer without violent resistance and voluntarily and courageously face death. Gandhi's closest associates in South Africa were frequently Jews, and he has great sympathy for the Jews.[1] He describes them historically as the untouchables of Christianity and he sympathizes with them as victims of Nazi genocide. However, most commentators conclude that Gandhi's advice is insensitive, ill informed, naive, out of touch, immoral and suicidal. In their correspondence the Jewish existentialist philosopher Martin Buber, who lived in Germany until 1938 and greatly admires Gandhi, points out that Gandhi's *satyagraha* advice ignores how the situation facing Jews in Germany is not comparable to that facing Indians in South Africa or India. It only has a chance of working when there is a witness. As with some other examples, one can wonder how the exemplary moral Gandhi can give such particular advice that can be seen as irrelevant and immoral.[2]

Gandhi's advice to the Jews, and even to Hitler in a letter of 23 July 1939, is especially significant since it is often used by critics to illustrate how Gandhi is completely irrelevant at best and complicit and enabling at worst.[3] As a way of dismissing Gandhi, critics most frequently refer to Hitler and the Nazis, to September 11, 2001 terrorists in New York or to 26 November 2008 terrorists in Mumbai. First, it is evident that Gandhi in the 1930s and 1940s is very isolated and insulated – focusing on constructive work, untouchability, Hindu–Muslim harmony, Quit India and other

India issues. Therefore he is very ill informed and uninformed about what is happening internationally in general and to European Jews in particular. Second, although Gandhi's short-term advice may be seen as naive and immoral, this need not undermine his major strength in raising the basic need for long-term, transformative, preventative nonviolent education, socialization and mobilization. One can analyse many ways that Gandhi's approach, if it had been embraced by the victorious Allies after the First World War or by the German people in the 1920s, could have prevented Hitler and the Nazis from coming to power. Third, as will be demonstrated, Gandhi, while upholding the absolute ideal of *ahimsa*, sometimes allows for the necessary use of violence when there are no nonviolent options that have a real possibility of being effective in countering the violence. In short, one can submit that a reformulated Gandhi approach today could view his advice to the European Jews as another 'Himalayan miscalculation'.[4]

The other source of controversy and numerous attacks focuses on Gandhi's approach to *brahmacharya* and his 'test' of chastity and purity.[5] While in Noakhali District in East Bengal Gandhi openly shares his intentions of sleeping with naked young women, especially with his grandniece Manu. Close associates, including Nirmal Kumar Bose, author of *My Days with Gandhi*, express disagreement and warn him that this will be scandalous. Several feel the need to withdraw from him in protest.[6] Although these experiments can be analysed in different ways, it is clear that Gandhi is not interested in sexual conquests or pleasure. For Gandhi these are not 'experiments' but more of a '*yagna*' ('*yajna*'), a sacrifice of his sexuality to God, which serves as a test of his chastity.

This 'sacrifice' of sexuality is a particular illustration of the central role of 'sacrifice' in Gandhi overall philosophy, practices and way of being in the world. Gandhi's essential use of 'sacrifice' is frequently misunderstood and his celebration of personal sacrifice is seen as bizarre and masochistic. For Gandhi, one must 'sacrifice' illusory, egotistic and violent passions, desires, attachments and goals in order to experience truth, real nonviolence and peace, true happiness and self-realization. Thus 'sacrifice' is essential for self-purification and moral and spiritual development that includes action-oriented transformative selfless service.

At this late date Gandhi is full of self-doubt and despair about the violence, hatred, communal disharmony and untruths all around him. What does this reveal about him? He has consistently upheld the position that a pure exemplary figure has a moral and spiritual potency. If others are acting so violently, Gandhi questions whether this is a reflection of own lack of sexual purity. In addition he embraces a traditional Indian position, shared by other spiritual approaches, that disciplined, perfected self-restraint, including sexual restraint, leads to self-purification and overcoming *karmic*, illusory, ego-directed blockages. This self-restraint taps into remarkable moral and spiritual energy that allows for focused selfless service, self-realization and freedom. In this sense, Gandhi repeatedly affirms that the perfected forces of nonviolence and truth are infallible and will always be victorious regardless of short-term defeats.

Therefore, for Gandhi, sleeping with the young women is really a test of his own purity and perfection. He disregards prudent advice, listening only to his own inner view or conscience and seems to conclude that he has maintained self-restraint and passed his purity test. This renews his confidence and faith in nonviolence as the only means for ending the raging communal violence in Noakhali, Bihar, Calcutta and Delhi. However, even if one gives Gandhi the benefit of the doubt, what remains troubling is that, as with some of his relations with his family and with others, Gandhi seems very self-centred in his individual experiments with truth, purity and nonviolence. He seems oblivious to the relational effects these have on others. In this case he does not seem sensitive to the fact that he is the revered Mahatma, that he has an authoritarian power relation with these young Gandhi devotees and that his personal experiments deeply affect the lives of other individuals. Once again, a reformulated Gandhi approach today could easily critique some of the positions he took on sexual tests and other matters.

Despite his diminished influence, the last period, when Gandhi is 77 and 78, from his visit to Noakhali toward the end of 1946 to his last fast in Delhi in January 1948, represents the most heroic stage of his entire life. In response to the Muslim League's Direct Action Day protest in August 1946 there are Muslim uprisings in Calcutta with riots and many killings. The communal rioting, death and suffering spread to other parts of India during the year before India's independence, especially to the Noakhali District of East Bengal, now in Bangladesh. In reaction to the Noakhali Genocide riots break out in Bihar toward the end of 1946. Rioting spreads to Punjab and the Northwest Frontier Province in late 1946 and early 1947. Where there is a Muslim majority, as in Bengal and Punjab, Hindus and often Sikhs suffer most from the rioting and massacres. Where there is a Hindu majority, as in Bihar, Muslims suffer most.

Some of the most heroic images are of the determined Gandhi, often walking barefooted 18 hours a day, from village to village in Noakhali, under the most difficult physical conditions, in hostile environments and with threats to his life. From October 1946 to February 1947 he visits 47 villages, listening patiently to the stories of atrocities and comforting victims. He skilfully intervenes to calm violent passions, spreads his message of love and reconciliation, organizes prayer sessions, gets villagers to take pledges to stop the killing and gradually restores some level of communal peace and harmony. He then spends several months in Hindu-dominated Bihar attempting once again, under very difficult and threatening conditions, to end the rioting and killings and to restore communal peace. It is astounding that Gandhi, often as one isolated individual

During Gandhi's courageous peace tour of Bihar with the nonviolent Pashtun leader Khan Abdul Gaffar Khan, known as the 'frontier Gandhi', behind him, 28 March 1947.

against all odds, could be so successful in ending violence, riots, calls for reprisals and genocidal killings and in restoring so much communal understanding, peace and harmony.

Yet Gandhi's heroic efforts cannot prevent the bloodbath in the period before and after India's Partition and Independence on 15 August 1947. Pakistan is created from the two regions with clear Muslim majorities: the northwest that becomes West Pakistan, now all of Pakistan, and the northeast that becomes East Pakistan, now Bangladesh. Although figures vary widely, it is estimated that at least one million people are slaughtered. Several million Hindus,

Muslims and Sikhs are turned into refugees. There are many debates over whether the Partition and one of the worst genocides in modern history could have been avoided. What is not debatable is how devastating the overwhelming hatred, violence and killings are to Gandhi, since they seem to refute his lifelong faith and commitment to truth and nonviolence. In late 1946 and 1947 he keeps making statements to the effect that he is 'being tested through and through' and he feels 'totally lost'. He states: 'All around me is utter darkness.' As he attempts to stop the killings, especially through fasts that bring him close to death, he states that he even welcomes death, since he can't bear to experience the killings and suffering all around him.

The Partition of India into two nations is a devastating blow to Gandhi. Having worked for over forty years for Muslim–Hindu unity, he never favours Partition, frequently stating that he will not be party to India's 'vivisection'. Finally, he concludes that he no longer has any influence with the British rulers, Jinnah and the majority of Muslims, and even Nehru and Patel, his closest associates in Congress. In June 1947 the Congress Working Committee reluctantly accepts the Viceroy Mountbatten Partition Plan as the only way to avoid Hindu–Muslim civil war. Gandhi, feeling helpless, does not oppose the plan, but this is far from real approval. This is evident when India's independence is proclaimed on 15 August in Delhi and Gandhi refuses to send the requested message of good wishes, feels no reason to celebrate and is far away doing the constructive work of trying to stop the killings and restore communal peace. For Gandhi, what India achieves in 1947 is not real independence in the sense of true *swaraj*. The new India exemplifies the limitations and evils of the violent modern nation state, simply substituting Indian for British rulers and power relations. It lacks the commitment to nonviolence and truth that is necessary for true self-reliance, the basis for individual and national freedom and independence.

At the time of India's independence, Gandhi is in Calcutta. He and the nation are shocked by the death and destruction in the city. The Muslim League and Bengal premier H. S. Suhrawardy urge Muslims to rise up. Hindus retaliate, and starting with the 'Great Calcutta Killing' on 16 August, many thousands are killed. Gandhi proposes to Suhrawardy that they share a Muslim house as a symbol of Hindu–Muslim unity. In the atmosphere of extreme communal hatred and violence Gandhi is verbally attacked as an enemy of Hindus, even physically attacked, and his life is seriously threatened. On the evening of 1 September Gandhi decides that he will fast until peace returns to Calcutta. The fast has an immediate effect with violence dying down, interreligious peace marches, others fasting, some turning in their weapons, and students and others questioning how Gandhi could die for their crimes. On 4 September Hindu Mahasabha, Sikh and Muslim League leaders come to Gandhi and ask him to end his fast. When they agree to Gandhi's condition that they pledge to risk their lives to prevent another recurrence of the killings and violence, he breaks his fast.

What Gandhi achieves in Calcutta, as chronicled by Pyarelel, Manu, N. K. Bose and others, is described as the 'Calcutta miracle'. Congress leader and close associate Chakravarti Rajagopalachari (C. R.) states that 'Gandhiji has achieved many things, but in my considered opinion, there has been nothing, not even independence, which is so truly wonderful as his victory over evil in Calcutta.'[7] Viceroy Mountbatten writes to Gandhi: 'In the Punjab we have 55 thousand soldiers and large scale rioting on our hands. In Bengal our forces consist of one man, and there is no rioting.'[8]

On the way to the Punjab, to try to stop the killings and violence, Gandhi decides to stop in Delhi where communal rioting is also raging. Under very dangerous conditions he visits terrified Muslims, distraught Hindu refugees from Pakistan and angry Hindu nationalist gatherings. Once again, in a dramatic move in desperate times, Gandhi decides on 13 January 1948 to undergo a fast unto death in order to restore Hindu–Muslim–Sikh unity and harmony. As he states: 'Death for me would be a glorious deliverance rather than that I should be a helpless witness to the destruction of India, Hinduism, Sikhism, and Islam.' In a very weakened state and suffering from ill health, Gandhi is close to death. Concerned Hindu, Muslim and Sikh leaders visit Gandhi at the Birla House and reassure him that they renounce violence and will work for peace.

During the Indo-Pakistani state of war, including the Pakistan-supported invasion of the princely State of Jammu and Kashmir in September, followed by the State's accession to the Indian Union and the deployment of Indian troops, the Government of India decided not to pay Pakistan the 55 crores (550 million Indian rupees) due as part of the Partition Council agreement. The Indian Government now reverses its decision and meets Gandhi's demand that it make the payment.[9]

On 18 January Gandhi breaks his fast. As in Noakhali, Bihar and Calcutta, Gandhi, through fasting and other efforts, works another 'miracle' as thousands stop the rioting and killing. Even people in Pakistan are moved by his sacrifice and suffering during the Delhi fast. Nevertheless, the situation in Delhi, the Punjab and elsewhere remains explosive and dangerous. Mobs have been chanting 'Death to Gandhi'. He receives death threats and a bomb explodes at his prayer meeting on 20 January. Gandhi senses that he may be killed but he refuses additional security measures.

Although in a weakened state of health after the fast and facing such threatening conditions, Gandhi somehow manages to tap into new energy with a determined will, and remains not only active but also experimentally creative during the last days of his life. He tentatively plans a bold visit to Pakistan set for February. On 29 January he writes about his radical ideas in a 'Constitutional Draft' for the Indian National Congress. Gandhi proposes that Congress dissolve itself as a political parliamentary organization and be reconstituted as a Lok Sevak Sangh (People's Servants' Association),

Mahatma Gandhi's earthly belongings.

working in every village on communal harmony, eradicating untouchability, improving employment and health care and realizing other aspects of the Constructive Programme. Such 'social, moral and economic independence' is the goal of true *swaraj*, real self-reliance and independence.

On 30 January Gandhi has a full day of visitors at the Birla House, including a meeting with Sardar Vallabhbhai Patel to discuss tensions between Nehru and Patel, the two strongest leaders in the government. After 5:00 p.m. he leaves, a little late, for the short walk to his daily prayer meeting. In the crowd is Nathuram Godse, an educated modern Hindu and editor of a Marathi journal in Poona, who earlier had been an admirer of Gandhi. He becomes a follower of Savarkar and identifies at different times with the Hindu Mahasabha and the Rashtriya Swayamsevak Sangh (RSS), two of the militant, Hindu nationalist groups that regard Gandhi as pro-Muslim and as an enemy of Hindu India. Gandhi's insistence on the payment to enemy Pakistan is the last straw. Godse participates in a carefully planned conspiracy to assassinate Gandhi. He greets Gandhi, bows in reverence and then fires three pistol shots at close range. Gandhi's final words are reported as 'Hey Ram' ('Oh Ram', sometimes translated as 'Oh God'), although this account has been questioned. Gandhi dies instantly.

Gandhi's assassination shocks India and the world and has the immediate effect of stopping much of the madness, rioting and killing and bringing India back from the brink of disaster. On 31 January Gandhi's body is cremated at Raj Ghat in New Delhi, site of the Mahatma Gandhi Memorial (or *Samadhi*). Later Godse and co-conspirator Narayan Apte are tried and convicted; they are executed on 15 November 1949.

Thus ends the extraordinary life of one of history's most remarkable human beings, so widely admired, even revered, and at the same time so controversial. On a personal level Gandhi has a fascinating personality and is an influential figure engaged in so many dramatic struggles and in shaping so many historical developments. But what is his greater lasting significance and relevance? What are his assumptions and theories, his model for exemplary character development and a life of integrity and the basis for his action-oriented transformative practices? How can we account for so much courage and perseverance, for ongoing experiments with truth and nonviolence and for his meaningful and significant way of being in the world? To answer these questions, we must go beyond Gandhi the particular individual and examine his basic moral and spiritual philosophy.

6

Gandhi's Philosophy: Truth and Nonviolence

From his youth until the very day of his assassination Gandhi's life is marked by his sincere, honest, dynamic and open-ended experiments with truth and nonviolence. He experiences a great diversity of situations that express values, relations and structures of oppression, exploitation, alienation, humanly caused suffering, violence and untruth. He always emphasizes the primacy of practice, and his analysis arises out of the particular, contextual, experiential world within which he is living. His experimental ideas are confirmed or falsified by testing them in terms of new practice. Gandhi is primarily a moralist, who focuses on the practical concerns of how we can be actively engaged in education, socialization, *satyagraha*, constructive work and a life of trans-formative practices so that we can live as virtuous individuals who are integral parts of virtuous societies.[1]

In this practical moral orientation Gandhi is not concerned with being a critical, systematic thinker who can offer abstract philoso-phical formulations. He is not overly concerned with theoretical consistency. When others point to his inconsistencies, he replies that he is not aware of being inconsistent, but if others find inconsistencies they should take his most recent formulations as most adequate. Gandhi, as he himself confesses, is certainly not a 'philosopher' in any critical, academic or scholarly sense.[2] However, his basic existential orientation or way of being in the world, his fundamental assumptions and values and commitments,

When asked for his philosophy, Gandhi frequently replied: 'My life is my message.'

and his theoretical formulations and diverse practices are philosophically challenging and insightful. Indeed, one could maintain that Gandhi is more philosophically interesting, significant and relevant than 90 per cent of what is done in contemporary 'professional' philosophy.

Many of Gandhi's admirers, during his lifetime and today, approach the Mahatma simply as a revered, awesome, idiosyncratic, mystical, larger-than-life, too-good-for-this world, moral and spiritual being. In addition, even most Gandhi admirers, citing such famous quotations as 'my life is my message', feel that following in the path of this remarkable individual M. K. Gandhi consists entirely in the practical task of simplifying one's needs, being peaceful and nonviolent and living a Gandhi-inspired life.

What is often overlooked is that in a dynamic, flexible, contextually sensitive, inclusive manner, Gandhi actually embraces a profound underlying theory or philosophy. Only by appreciating this moral and spiritual philosophy of truth and nonviolence can one understand why Gandhi engages in particular practices, what motivates and sustains him, why he assesses experimental practices as successes or failures and how a reformulated Gandhian philosophy may have great significance and relevance today.

Gandhi's two major philosophical concepts are *satya* (truth, which he uses interchangeably with God, self, soul) and *ahimsa* (nonviolence, avoiding harm, noninjury, which he uses interchangeably with love). Although Gandhi is best known for his nonviolence, one cannot understand his views and practices of nonviolence without understanding his analysis of truth and the integral relation of truth and nonviolence.

In his view of reality, Gandhi emphasizes the metaphysical or ontological concept of truth that focuses on *sat*, that which really exists (what is real, being, the true essence). It is revealing that Gandhi entitles his autobiography 'the story of my experiments with truth'. His life of challenging varied experiences reveals his determination to pursue truth no matter where it takes him. This unending pursuit of truth necessitates an incredibly strong will, self-reflection and self-purification, courage, fearlessness, sacrifice and voluntary suffering. This pursuit often involves taking positions that are unpopular and disturbing, challenge those with privilege and power and place Gandhi's life at great risk.

One major difficulty in formulating Gandhi's view of truth or reality is that he is so inclusive, flexible and eclectic. As Gandhi states: 'For me the Voice of God, of Conscience, of Truth or the Inner Voice or the still small Voice mean one and the same thing.'[3] His own spiritual positions on truth and reality range from very personal devotional affirmations to Rama and other deities to very impersonal Vedantic affirmations of some impersonal, all-pervading, absolute spiritual force or power. He usually presents positions in which truth or God is interchangeable with morality, and a nonreligious person can identify with his approach to reality. In other passages his approach to truth or God is greatly dependent on personal faith and divine grace. At times Gandhi submits that he prefers a monistic, *Advaita* (pure nondualistic) view of reality, but then says that he also believes in a non-*Advaita* view of reality of oneness with differences, or that he upholds a supernatural view of God or deities that is rejected by pure nondualism. Scholars and other commentators debate to what extent Gandhi's formulations of truth, as well as of nonviolence and other key concepts, are muddle-headed, inconsistent and incoherent and to what extent they are eclectic, pluralistic, insightful and open-ended in a helpful innovative way for dealing with issues of violence, war, suffering, domination and civilizational disharmony.

When it comes to Gandhi's attitude toward others, the difficulty in formulating his philosophy of reality is even greater. He will often share his view of truth but then advise others that they must do their own experiments and pursue truth no matter where it takes them. What is true for Gandhi may not be true for them. And yet Gandhi is determined to avoid a pluralism that results in the acceptance of unlimited subjective and relativistic positions. He can accept a certain kind of descriptive relativism in the sense that different religions and cultures express different approaches to and formulations of reality, even if he maintains that these are different relative paths to and formulations of the same Ultimate Reality or Absolute Truth. However, he never endorses a normative relativism that to assert that x is true can mean nothing more than x is true for y within society or culture z. Hatred, torture, terrorism, exploitation, involuntary poverty and suffering may seem to some to be justified, moral and socially and religiously sanctioned, but they are always immoral, evil and are based on untruths and false views of reality.[4]

There is no God
but Truth
2 · 4 · '39   mkgandhi

Gandhi teaching his philosophy of Reality as Truth that he often equates with God, 1939.

In various writings Gandhi reports that at an earlier stage in his life he defined reality in terms of 'God' and accepted the traditional, theistic view of 'God is truth', in which truth is one of the many essential attributes of God. He later emphasizes the significance of his reformulated view of reality in terms of the key concept of truth, reversing his previous formulation to a more inclusive

'Truth is God'. Such a broader philosophical approach could then encompass Jains, Buddhists, atheists, secular humanists and others who strive for truth but do not adopt God-formulations.[5]

While acknowledging and even celebrating the diversity of his and other formulations of truth and reality Gandhi sometimes shares his personal preference for the impersonal, nondualistic, spiritual view of *Brahman* that is expressed in key Hindu Upanishadic passages. Reminiscent of such Vedic expressions of a view of reality in terms of an all-encompassing, permanent, spiritual Self, Gandhi often writes of truth or God as an impersonal Absolute, an unseen power or unifying force pervading all things, pure consciousness, the changeless essence of life beyond name and form.

> There is an indefinable mysterious Power that pervades everything. I feel It, though I do not see It. It is this unseen Power which makes Itself felt and yet defies all proof, because It is so unlike all that I perceive through my senses. It transcends the senses . . . I do dimly perceive that whilst everything around me is ever changing, ever dying, there is underlying all that change a living Power that is changeless, that holds all together, that creates, dissolves and recreates. That informing Power or Spirit is God. And since nothing else I see merely through the senses can or will persist, He alone is.[6]

Consistent with the Vedic Upanishadic and Advaitin monistic identification of *Brahman* (Reality, Being) with *Atman* (the Self), Gandhi often uses the terms Truth, God and Self interchangeably.

Gandhi's inclusive and pluralistic approach to reality includes different formulations of self, soul and self-other relations. First, Gandhi often affirms the true moral and spiritual self in terms of an inner individual essence, sometimes expressed as 'an inner voice', conscience or the God within each of us. Second, Gandhi most commonly affirms the true self as social and relational. His understanding of the Hindu concept of *dharma* or ethical and social obligation shapes this view and it can be related to Confucian and other Asian relational formulations: I am self only in relation to the other; the relational other is an essential part of my self-identity. Third, Gandhi affirms his preference for the impersonal, universal unifying, pure Absolute self or soul that can be identified with the Hindu *Atman*. These self and self–other formulations are often complementary, but they also express ambiguities, tensions, contradictions and unresolved philosophical problems and issues.[7]

As Bhikhu Parekh has analysed, Gandhi's view of self focuses on his emphasis on *swabhava* or our individual, unique, physical, mental and social nature and contextual situatedness.[8] This is a dynamic approach in which we are born into this world with our own nature and then develop and realize our individual self-nature through our social interactions and relations with others. Although Gandhi has many general or universal values he rejects a rigid absolute view of human nature. He repeatedly advises others to be true to their own, unique, changing nature by understanding and acting in ways reflecting their individual self. This focus on the individual self with its unique nature should not be confused with the atomistic, modern, Western ego-oriented individual and ideology of individualism.

Although Gandhi sometimes expresses his personal preference for an Advaita Vedanta monistic interpretation of the pure, undifferentiated, impersonal, nondualistic, spiritual Absolute Self, he is not consistent in his formulations of Truth, God and Self. The above passage about his experience of the unseen permanent Power or Spirit need not commit one to nondualism, and his identification of such a spiritual Truth or Reality with 'God' and 'He' is not a formulation consistent with the pure nondualistic monism. One can certainly provide a Hindu neo-Vedantic interpretation of some of Gandhi's philosophy, but he is not a traditional Advaitin or traditional Vedantist of any variety. This is because Gandhi is a philosophical realist, and he tries to integrate his realism with a specific kind of pragmatic idealism. As will be seen, this means that Gandhi resists devaluing and dismissing this world as *maya* or illusion and places primary emphasis on relative truth and relative nonviolence. He claims, in a nontraditional way, that no one knows Truth, God or Self, and even he has only fleeting, imperfect 'glimpses' of Absolute Truth and Absolute Nonviolence.

At this point, we need only emphasize the ontological claim in Gandhi's approach to truth: there exists some deeper, permanent spiritual power or force that allows us to experience the meaningful interrelatedness and unity of all reality. Gandhi presents an inclusive, organic, holistic philosophical approach with presuppositions and principles that affirm the essential unity and interrelatedness of all existence, the indivisibility of truth that is manifested in diverse ways and the integral relation of truth and nonviolence.

Gandhi's second major philosophical concept is *ahimsa* or nonviolence. As the best known and most significant modern theorist and practitioner of nonviolence, nothing is more important for analysing and responding to contemporary conflict, war, suffering and civilizational disharmony than understanding Gandhi's insightful approach to violence. Gandhi deepens and broadens our use of the terms 'violence' and 'nonviolence'. He challenges us to rethink how our ordinary uses of 'nonviolence' are very 'violent' and our ordinary uses of 'peace' usually express states of conflict, disharmony and war.

In standard dictionaries 'violence' has two kinds of meanings. First, it is defined as a force that is intense, immoderate, fierce and rough. Second, there are definitions with a clear negative meaning: 'violence' is a fierce and rough force that involves aggression, assault, infringement and violation. For Gandhi nonviolence, like violence, is a force, but without being a rough force that involves aggression and violation. Unlike most other approaches that view nonviolence as simply being against something (not violent) and as passive (refraining from exercising violent force), Gandhi's *ahimsa* is an active, positive, moral, truthful, transformative force. Most people claim to be against violence and war and for nonviolence and peace, but they use these terms in a very narrow sense. We restrict 'violence' and 'war' to overt physical forces and conflicts. 'Violence' refers to killing, assaults, rape, torture, domestic physical abuse, bullying and terrorist attacks. 'War' involves military attacks, shooting, bombing and threatening with military force. In this sense conflict resolution and peace-building involve the challenge of how to transform or prevent these overt, physical, violent conflicts.

In his profound philosophy of *ahimsa* and throughout his life Gandhi is very concerned with illustrations of brute overt violent force and overt armed conflicts of war. His approach is insightful for providing transformative methods for conflict resolution with regard to physical assaults, shootings, bombings, torture, rape, bullying and other clear examples of the violent infliction of suffering on others. However, such serious, overt, physical acts are only a relatively small part of overall violence, and Gandhi broadens and deepens our understanding of violence in two main ways.

First, Gandhi frequently addresses the multidimensionality of violence. In addition to overt physical violence Gandhi often points to inner or psychological, linguistic, economic, social, political, cultural, religious and educational violence. Numerous manifestations of such multidimensional violence are not overt but express themselves in concealed and camouflaged ways. Such violence is often expressed in states of multidimensional war and war-making, such as economic, psychological, cultural and religious war. We are socialized and educated in such ways that all of these dimensions of violence interact, mutually reinforce each other and lead to a violent, disharmonious, 'normal' world view in which we relate violently to ourselves, to others and to nature.

To examine very briefly only one dimension of violence, Gandhi, unlike most philosophers and others who adopt ethical and spiritual approaches, places a primary emphasis on basic material needs and the 'normal' state of economic violence. You do not preach the higher virtues of nonviolence, peace, freedom, true *swaraj* or self-rule and independence to those who are impoverished and starving. To do so would be not only unrealistic and irrelevant but also immoral. Instead it is your duty to engage in selfless service working with others to provide meaningful work that results in food, water, shelter, health care and other basic material necessities without which a more developed ethical and spiritual life of truth and nonviolence is impossible.[9]

Repeatedly and in very contemporary ways Gandhi uses 'violence' as synonymous with economic exploitation. Gandhi is attentive to unequal, asymmetrical, violent power relations. A minority who possess and control wealth, capital, land and natural resources, technology and media are able to exploit and dominate those lacking such economic power. Gandhi identifies with starving and impoverished human beings and with the plight of peasants, workers and others disempowered, exploited and dominated.

Gandhi is very attentive to the growing concentration of wealth and power and the growing inequality between the haves and the have-nots in India and throughout the world. He emphasizes that such economic violence – including poverty, which he often describes as the worst form of violence – is not the result of super-natural design or immutable law of nature. It involves humanly caused oppression, exploitation, domination, injustice and suffering and, hence, we as human beings are responsible. If I could change conditions and alleviate suffering but I choose either to profit from such economic violence or not to get involved, I perpetuate, am complicit with and am responsible for the economic violence of the status quo. Obviously, incorporating such concerns of economic violence broadens and radically changes the causal analysis and understanding of the nature of true nonviolence, peace and civilizational and environmental harmony.

Mention of the economic violence of the status quo points to Gandhi's second innovative way for broadening and deepening the perspective on violence: his emphasis on the structural violence of the status quo. This is 'business as usual' or simply the way things are, which we usually don't even recognize as violent. For Gandhi the normal dominant economic, political, cultural, religious and educational systems are inherently violent. They assume views of human nature, rationality, success, happiness and progress that express multidimensional violent relations toward one's self, others and nature. The fact that the dominant system seems to be functioning efficiently, without examples of overt physical violence and disruption, creates an illusion of nonviolence.

For thousands of years and continuing today human beings have suffered and died without responding with active noncooperation, protests and resistance. They typically accept and adjust to their oppressive relations because they accept their unfortunate conditions as 'that's life' and the way things have always been and will be; they feel fearful, hopeless and powerless to change their situation; they blame themselves for their suffering and often accept some religious or other ideological explanation and justification for their situation. But such typical understandable responses must not disguise or minimize the structural violence of the status quo. As Gandhi repeatedly emphasizes, if people are dominated, exploited and oppressed, but suffer passively and without overt violent reaction, that is a very violent situation that creates a false sense of peace and nonviolence.

In Gandhi's approach to the structural violence of the status quo, constructive nonviolent disruption, sometimes involving seemingly 'unpeaceful' conflict, plays a crucial role. In Gandhi's *satyagraha* and other nonviolent methods of resistance, active intervention, creative tension and transformative disruption are often necessary for exposing, raising consciousness and transforming the structural violence of the status quo. Gandhi uses a medical image for analysing and transforming the 'normal' relational system of multidimensional violence. It's as if the patient is unaware of a deep serious illness, such as cancer. Pointing to the cancer will often produce discomfort, self-denial and anger, and will certainly disrupt one's normal life, but this is necessary to cure the disease and regain health. For Gandhi our status quo or dominant economic, technological, social, cultural, psychological, political, state, military, media, religious, environmental, educational, civilizational structures and relations are unhealthy, alienating, violent and unsustainable. These dominant structural relations are increasingly deadly, like a cancer, threatening human existence and life on planet earth. But Gandhi is both an optimist and a philosophical realist and he maintains that this unhealthy state of our present existence in the world is 'curable' if we adopt the transformative means and ends of nonviolence and truth.

In Gandhi's philosophy of truth and nonviolence, central to any relevant Gandhian perspective, *satya* and *ahimsa* must be brought into an integral, dialectical, mutually interacting and reinforcing relation.[10] Most often Gandhi presents *satya* as the end and *ahimsa* the means. We cannot use violent means to achieve truthful ends. In the means–ends ethical analysis, immoral violent means lead to immoral, violent, untruthful ends. Gandhi also states that the ideals of *ahimsa* and *satya* are convertible or interchangeable as means and ends. As we have seen, nonviolence is the means for realizing the truth. As we are educated and socialized to become more nonviolent, we become more truthful. However, truth is also a means for becoming more loving and nonviolent. Living more truthfully is an essential part of the developmental process for living more nonviolently. As we become more educated and socialized as to the true nature of reality we resist living under false illusions of violence and hatred.

However, with his major ethical focus, readers and even most followers usually overlook the key point that Gandhi is also making a major ontological claim in relating truth and nonviolence. Nonviolence is a powerful bonding and unifying force that brings us together in caring, loving, cooperative relations, that allows us to realize and act consistently with the interconnectedness and unity of all of life. Violence, by way of contrast, maximizes ontological separateness and divisiveness, and is based on the fundamental belief that the other – whether individual, class, caste, gendered, racial, ethnic, religious or national target of my hatred and violence – is essentially different from me or us. In other words, in the Gandhian perspective, violence and hatred are not only unethical but are also inconsistent with truth and reality, whereas nonviolence and love are the ethical means for realizing truth and reality.

Only by understanding the nature of truth and nonviolence and their integral, mutually reinforcing relations can we understand how we are socialized and educated in ways that prevent us from realizing the reality or truth of the unity and interrelatedness of life, and from realizing and living consistently with the reality of nonviolence and love. Gandhi's philosophy and practices offer ways for resisting pervasive forms of violence and untruth and for proposing positive alternatives that are grounded in *satya* (truth), *ahimsa* (nonviolence), *satyagraha* ('firmness for the truth', truth-force, love-force, soul-force), *swadharma* (one's own duty), *swadeshi* (self-sufficient economy based on one's local or national products), *sarvodaya* (the well-being of all) and real *swaraj* (self-rule, self-government). An expanded consciousness of a more complex, nuanced, overt and hidden, holistic, relational approach to violence and war radically changes how we understand and respond to our contemporary crises and how we transform violent structures and relations into ones of truth, nonviolence, love, compassion and self-rule.

In his philosophy Gandhi introduces several key concepts for analysing and bringing about this transformation toward greater nonviolence and truth. These include his significant analysis of the integral relations of means and ends; his key short-term and especially long-term preventative approach to violence; and his brilliant analysis of the relative–absolute distinction in which he affirms absolute regulative ideals, but emphasizes that we at most have 'glimpses' of the Absolute and are always at best moving from one, imperfect, relative state of violence and nonviolence to greater, imperfect realizations of relative truth and nonviolence.

As Gandhi repeatedly maintains, Hobbesian and most other modern perspectives involve versions of the doctrine that the ends justify the means. Violence is necessarily used in the name of nonviolence. War and war-making are used in the name of peace and peacebuilding. Gandhi claims that such modern approaches are foundationally and structurally unethical. They express means–ends systems of violent values and relations that can only produce violent versions of 'freedom', 'independence', 'security' and 'peace' that perpetuate violent states of unfreedom, dependence, insecurity and war.

A key to Gandhi's alternative preventative approach to violence and war is his famous analysis of means and ends. He analyses the integral, moral, means–ends relations, allowing us to decondition the multidimensional violent causes and structures and interject compassionate, loving, truthful, nonviolent causal factors and structures to break the vicious endless cycles of violence and war.

Gandhi rejects contemporary positions that maintain that economic, political and other ends justify the means. He rejects utilitarianism's principle of 'the greatest happiness of the greatest number' and other modern formulations of 'national independence', 'security', 'democracy' and other seemingly noble ends used to justify violent unethical means and sacrifice millions of human beings. Instead, Gandhi embraces a philosophy of *sarvodaya* ('the welfare of all'). [11] With his emphasis on the pure moral will and ethical intentions, it is tempting to consider Gandhi an anti-consequentialist Kantian or deontologist, but this also is an inadequate classification. As seen throughout his life, Gandhi often has the best of intentions, but if his experiments with truth lead to undesirable results, he assesses them as failures. Here we see that Gandhi emphasizes both means and ends and their integral, mutually reinforcing relations. Although Gandhi describes himself as a pragmatic idealist who is concerned with ethical and spiritual results, he places even greater emphasis on nonviolent moral means. This is because we often have much greater control over the means we use, whereas noble ends, such as ending war and violence, may be unattainable because they express ideals beyond our power of realization.

Although we may be tempted to use violent means for short-term benefits, Gandhi repeatedly emphasizes that we cannot use violence to overcome violence and achieve nonviolence. Violent impure means will shape violent impure ends regardless of our moralistic, self-justifying slogans and ideology.

In language similar to formulations of the law of *karma*, Gandhi warns us that economic, psychological and other forms of violence lead to more violence, and we become entrapped in endless vicious cycles of escalating violence and war. For Gandhi, as for the Buddha, most violence has a moral character and involves intention and choice. It is this moral character of volitional intention and choice that binds us to the vicious cycles of violence, war and suffering. This can also be related to Gandhi's identification with the *Gita*'s action path of *karma yoga* in which one's intentional attitude of nonattachment to the results of one's action is key to breaking the *karmic* attachment to results. The only way to move toward more nonviolent ends is to assume a nonviolent attitude and to introduce nonviolent causal factors through the adoption of nonviolent means. Such nonviolent factors will begin to weaken the causal factors that produce violent chain reactions that keep us trapped in destructive cycles of violence.

In many respects Gandhi's perspective of means–ends preventative analysis is similar to the Buddha's formulation of the Doctrine of Dependent Origination (*pratitya-samutpada* or Pali *paticca-samuppada*). Violence, terror, exploitation, greed, hatred and war are not independent, eternal, absolute or inevitable. They exist within a violent phenomenal world of impermanent, interdependent relativity. Historical, psychological, economic, social, religious and other forms of violence are caused and conditioned, and themselves become causes and condition other violent consequences that then become new violent causal factors that fuel our state of violence and war. The path of *ahimsa* involves focusing on the means that allow you to decondition such violent causal factors and conditions and to introduce nonviolent causes and conditions that will lead to more nonviolent results, of greater peace and security, that will then become new causal factors. This means–ends relation involves mutual interaction, since the adoption of nonviolent ideals, as ends, will also have a causal influence on shaping appropriate nonviolent means. This very process of means–ends causal transformation, by which one transforms relations with others in order to serve their real needs, unmet in the violent relations of domination, exploitation and war, is the very process by which one transforms one's own self toward greater freedom, real peace, real security and self-realization.

In his analysis of means–ends relations Gandhi offers his greatest strength for dealing with violence, war, injustice, exploitation and alienation: nonviolent preventative measures for long-term changes necessary for identifying and transform-ing root causes and causal determinants that keep us trapped in escalating cycles of violence. However, it is important to emphasize that a Gandhian perspective also has profound short-term nonviolent and peace-building benefits.

Gandhi offers many possibilities for short-term conflict resolution when contradictions become exacerbated, and individuals, groups or nations are on the brink of overt violence and war. Gandhi's own life is replete with illustrations of how he is able to intervene through listening, sympathizing, engaged dialogue, fasting, willingness to suffer and other forms of nonviolent intervention and resistance in order to defuse very tense, violent situations.

If someone intent on inflicting violence confronts me, Gandhi offers many responses that may prove effective in preventing violence. If I manage to limit my ego, achieve a larger perspective, do not define the other as 'enemy' and empathize with the other's feelings, this may allow for dialogue and for creating nonthreatening relations. In addition Gandhi repeatedly emphasizes that intellectual approaches with rational analysis often have no transformative effect on the other, but approaches of the heart, involving deep personal emotions and feelings, frequently have profound, relational, transformative effects. If I refuse to strike back and am willing to embrace sacrifice and suffering, this can disrupt the expectations of the violent other, lead to a decentring and reorienting of an extremely violent situation and touch the other's heart. Throughout his writings on *satyagraha* and other methods for resisting and transforming violence, Gandhi proposes numerous ways for relating to short-term violence and moving toward conflict resolution and peacebuilding grounded in truth and nonviolence.

The much greater strength of Gandhi's approach to violence involves long-term preventative education, socialization, relations and interventions so that we do not reach the stage of explosive overt violence and war. For Gandhi, over 90 per cent of violence is humanly caused, contingent and hence preventable. The greatest challenge is to identify root causes and basic causal determinants of violence and war and to propose alternative nonviolent determinants. This allows us to break escalating causal cycles of violence and war.

Gandhi places a high priority on education as essential to preventative approaches. Through education he deepens and broadens the analysis of violence, including educational violence, and the analysis of means–ends relations for getting at root causes and conditions underlying multidimensional violence. He devotes much time and effort to a radically different model of education with emphasis on character-building and moral and spiritual development. Education must focus on psychological awareness and analysis of how we constitute and must decondition ego-driven selfishness and greed, defence mechanisms responding to fear and insecurity, hatred, aggression and other violent intentions and inner states of consciousness that trap us in violent relations toward other classes, castes, genders, religions and nations. Education must focus on political, cultural, social, economic, linguistic, religious and other aspects of overall socialization that contribute to, tolerate and justify violence, oppression, exploitation and war.

The value of a long-term preventative Gandhian perspective can be illustrated by the very example frequently cited to refute Gandhi's approach to violence and war: how would Gandhi have dealt with Hitler? In this case we are not just dealing with some hypothetical question. We know of the letter that Gandhi wrote to Hitler on 23 March 1939, and we know what advice he gave to European Jews as they faced the immediate threat of genocide.[12] As was noted in chapter Five, although there is room for inter-pretation, disagreement and debate, Gandhi's short-term advice is uninformed, naive, ineffective and, at times, even unethical and suicidal. As will be seen, contemporary Gandhian perspectives are capable of providing radically different responses in such violent situations, even occasionally upholding the need for short-term violence in the name of peace and nonviolence.

It is not as if a Gandhian approach to Hitler has no short-term options. For example, even after Hitler and the Nazis came to power, if a majority of 'good Germans' had been morally, politically and spiritually concerned and had used a variety of nonviolent acts of noncooperation, the Nazis would have been greatly disempowered and the regime would have found it difficult to carry out its violent intentions and actions. Even if a significant minority of concerned, dedicated, nonviolently disciplined Germans had engaged in noncooperation, acts of resistance, with a willingness to suffer, this might have awakened the consciousness and conscience of many other citizens, touched their hearts and motivated them not to benefit from or become complicit with the violence being perpetuated in their name. Nevertheless, it must be conceded that at a certain point in history, especially after Hitler was appointed Chancellor on 30 January 1933, Gandhi's short-term efforts, as well as non-Gandhian approaches, had little chance of stopping the Nazi rise to power and violent devastation.

What is most instructive in this difficult Hitler and Nazi counter-example is the tremendous potential of Gandhi's long-term preventative approach. As is evident from the means–ends analysis, the rise to power of Hitler and the Nazis is not inevitable, but is causally determined by explicit and implicit, overt and hidden, multidimensional and structural violent relations. If Germans in the 1920s had had a more Gandhian sense of non-violent education, socialization, sensitivity to anti-Semitism and other forms of racism and persecution, less egoism and more concern for serving the needs of oppressed others and more motivation to intervene actively to expose and resist violent intentions, words and actions, one could prepare a long list of numerous things they could have done that would have prevented the relatively small number of Nazis from later rising to power. Similarly, one can think of numerous things the victorious Allies could have done differently, after the incredible death and suffering of the First World War, to arrive at a long-term preventative peace treaty, informed by a sense of restorative justice and peacebuilding reconciliation. Such an approach would have lessened the punishment and humiliation of Germany and would have gone a long way toward defusing or eliminating the subsequent causal factors that Hitler and the Nazis exploited in rising to power and justifying their violence and war-making at home and abroad.

In short, Gandhi's long-term preventative approach could have been very effective in preventing Hitler and the Nazis from coming to power and confronting the world with the difficult challenges of extreme short-term violence and war-making. It is such long-term preventative approaches that have the greatest potential for more permanent nonviolence and peacebuilding.

This brings us to Gandhi's usually overlooked analysis of dynamic relations between the absolute and the relative that is essential for providing a more nuanced, complex and adequate nonviolent approach. The key absolute–relative distinction and analysis challenges contemporary antithetical responses to violence and nonviolence, war-making and peacebuilding, that emphasize either unlimited cultural contextual relativism of values or narrow intolerant absolutism that imposes a supposedly universal model of human rights and peace on diverse others. A Gandhian perspective, by way of contrast, submits that such common, dichotomous formulations of absolute or relative truth, violence and nonviolence are inadequate, and that a more adequate dialectical analysis of the relative and the absolute is needed.

Gandhi himself sometimes conveys the impression that he is a simple, rigid, uncompromising absolutist with respect to violence, nonviolence, war, peace, vows, principles and rules, and other ethical and spiritual concepts and values. Gandhian perspectives focusing exclusively on such passages lead to dogmatic absolutist claims and ways of being in the world that are not sensitive to changing historical and contextual developments and that are often irrelevant when confronting violent challenges.

One can simply assert, for example, that the Mahatma would have been against contemporary dominant globalization and that is certainly true. Nevertheless, we live in a globalized world that is not going away and that largely defines the nature of violence and war-making today. A more adequate and more relevant Gandhi-informed perspective, while incorporating a strong critique of contemporary globalization, would explore how a Gandhian approach would constructively engage our world of globalized relations and what a radically different Gandhian formulation of globalization might look like in terms of bottom-up, decentralized, egalitarian, nonviolent relational theory and practice.

A more comprehensive examination of Gandhi's writings reveals a more subtle, nuanced and flexible Gandhi, who addresses the complexity of violence, struggles with linguistic, psychological and other forms of violence, and recognizes the difficulty of resolving violent conflicts and contradictions in human relations. This recognition of complexity in real situations of violent conflict and war-making must not minimize Gandhi's commitment to such absolutes as nonviolence, love and truth. Gandhi's philosophy, embracing such absolute ideals, resists certain fashionable modern approaches of unlimited facile relativism, complete subjectivism or postmodernist interpretations in which Gandhi's philosophy of nonviolence is nothing more than the construction of a Gandhi narrative without any claims to truth and reality.

As we have seen, Gandhi frequently emphasizes the two major absolutes of truth and nonviolence and how they must be brought into integral, mutually interacting and reinforcing relations. With this foundation of absolute truth and nonviolence it is tempting to formulate Gandhi's approach to violence in oversimplified and false ways by overlooking his emphasis on the following methodological, epistemological and ontological claim: all of us exist in this world as relative, finite, imperfect beings of limited, situated, embodied consciousness. Ambiguity, contradiction, fallibility and existential tension are defining aspects of our human mode of being in the world. Our knowledge is always conditioned, imperfect and perspectival. As Gandhi repeatedly states, even he, at most, has limited temporary 'glimpses' of absolute truth and nonviolence. A Gandhian approach, with ethical and spiritual paths of human development and self-realization, expresses the attempt to move from one relative truth and nonviolence to greater relative truth and nonviolence closer to the absolute regulative ideals.[13]

Here one finds the central place of empathy, care, mutuality, cooperation, tolerance and respect in Gandhi's nonviolent truthful approach. One of the most arrogant and dangerous moves – as seen in the ethnocentrism of many modern models and approaches to violence and war-making – is to make what is relative into an absolute. Recognizing the specificity and complexity of our con-textualized situatedness, a Gandhian perspective allows us to grasp relative partial truths. Our approach should be tolerant and open to other points of view; others have different relative perspectives and different glimpses of truth that we do not have. With relative limited knowledge we often misjudge situations and even misjudge our motives and that is why we must learn from our errors and from others in the movement toward greater truth and nonviolence. At the same time, as has been seen, Gandhi's nonviolent approach does not advocate uncritical absolute tolerance and passive acceptance of approaches based on multiple forms of violence and the violence of the status quo.

The absolute–relative distinction also allows one to address the most difficult challenges to Gandhi and any Gandhian approaches to violence. These frequently given anti-Gandhi refutations – such as how to respond when terrorists are slaughtering innocent people or napalm or bombs are being dropped, when madmen are killing people or rapes are taking place, when deadly animals or insects are threatening human life – usually consist of examples of extreme, erupting or immediate violence in which all of Gandhi's short-term and long-term preventative measures seem completely ineffective and irrelevant.

Consider the example most frequently used to refute Gandhi after the 9/11 terrorist attacks in 2001 in the United States and the 26/11 terrorist attacks in 2008 in Mumbai. Using the Mumbai illustration, sceptical questioners ask: what would Gandhi have done about the 26/11 terrorists? Such questioners are not focusing on long-term Gandhian preventative measures, which are the most significant and relevant for getting at root causes and transforming causal determinants that trap us in escalating cycles of violence and terror. They focus on the situation of 26/11 terrorists at the Chhatrapati Shivaji Terminus (CST, or Victoria Terminus, VT, train station), the Trident hotel, the Taj Mahal Palace and Tower hotel, the Leopold Café and the Jewish Chabad Nariman House. Terrorists are slaughtering innocent human beings. What immediate response does Gandhi's perspective advocate?

Most people who raise this difficult question assume that there is contemporary terrorism, on the one hand, and Gandhi's philosophy and practices, on the other hand, and the two have nothing to do with each other. In this sense Gandhi is irrelevant when responding to terrorists. In even stronger terms of refutation, anti-Gandhi questioners often assume that, at best, Gandhi may be well intentioned, but he is naive, ineffective and hence irrelevant, or, at worst, his nonviolent approach is complicit with, contributes to and is part of the problem of terrorism, since it weakens us by insisting that we not use violent force, the only means that can stop terrorists. When questioners complete their terrorist example of refutation, they often have a pronounced smirk or puffed-up self-assurance and confidence that they have demolished Gandhi and the Gandhian perspective.

However, an open-ended, flexible, self-critical, innovative Gandhian response to the terrorist refutation, using the key absolute–relative distinction, usually meets with initial surprise and then with curiosity and interest. Even many sceptics are then willing to engage in dialogue and often grant the soundness and potential of Gandhi's response. This is especially the case if one is modest in advocating Gandhi's perspective to such an immediate eruption of violence and terrorism and the need to combine this approach with other, complementary, non-Gandhian perspectives.

Largely because of uninformed stereotypes and simple slogans, even among some Gandhians, people do not realize that there are many passages in which Gandhi, while upholding the absolute ideal of *ahimsa*, grants the necessity of relative violence. In numerous passages he claims that for those who are not at a sufficient moral and spiritual level of development, brave ethically motivated acts of violence are to be preferred to passive cowardly 'nonviolence', which is furthest from true *ahimsa* and allows for the perpetuation of violence. Clearly this is relevant to how people could have responded to ongoing 26/11 acts of terrorism.[14]

In other writings Gandhi grants that even morally and spiritually developed human beings, because of their relative existential situation in the world, inevitably, unavoidably and often unintentionally are involved in some violence and destruction of life. This even applies to Gandhi's vegetarian diet and the application of disinfectants and other hygienic practices.[15]

More surprising, in terms of stereotypes of Gandhi's philosophy with his absolute commitment to *ahimsa*, is his view that there are unavoidable cases in which we may be required to use necessary relative violence in the cause of nonviolence. In contrast to a common stereotype Gandhi is not rendered passive and reduced to inaction when there is no effective nonviolent response. He would not simply allow the violent acts of Mumbai terrorists to take place. We act, using violent means if necessary, to prevent extreme violence because that is the least violent, most effective, contextualized response possible. Gandhi goes so far as to write about extreme cases under such titles as 'when killing may be *ahimsa*'![16]

In no way should Gandhi's approach be confused with the usual justifications for 'necessary' military, economic and other forms of violence and terrorism as part of the dominant modern ideologies of globalization and other modern violent structural and institutional responses. For Gandhi almost all of our violence is humanly caused, either actively or through nonresistance and complicity, and hence contingent; does not reflect a last resort since there are usually many nonviolent options; and is potentially preventable through short-term and long-term measures. This is the case even when we struggle with difficult issues of applying *ahimsa* to our relative contextual situatedness. However, even in cases in which violence is taking places and there are no nonviolent options, we must not misinterpret Gandhi's position.

Gandhi never rejects or deviates from the absolute of *ahimsa*, even when we have exhausted nonviolent options and he reluctantly grants the necessity of using violence to avoid much greater violence. One needs to intervene, perhaps even violently, to stop the Mumbai terrorists in the act of shooting innocent human beings, since no nonviolent intervention, including a willingness to die, has any possibility of stopping the killing. We use violent force to stop the terrorists, to disarm and capture them or, if necessary, to kill them. However, we must never glorify such relative violence that may be necessary, but is never moral and is always 'sinful'. It is tragic since it represents human failure in realizing more ethical and spiritual relations closer to the absolutes of truth and nonviolence. That we live in a world of violence, terror, hatred, exploitation and injustice is an indication of human failure. That we are forced to use violence is also an indication of human failure. We have failed to create preventative nonviolent structures, relations and conditions and to take nonviolent actions that could have avoided the need for such violence.

Always attempting to express our intentions, means and goals as informed by our absolute ideals of truth and nonviolence, we must limit the need for such relative necessary violence. We must restrict to the minimum the intensity and duration of such violence, feel saddened by such violence and work toward reconciliation. Most importantly for future nonviolence and peace-building, we must do everything possible to change violent and untruthful conditions and human relations in order to avoid the repetition of such tragic violence.

7

Modern Civilization, Religion and a New Paradigm

When it comes to philosophy and religion, M. K. Gandhi is primarily a moral thinker and practitioner who is always concerned with how human beings actually live their lives. He is more focused on practical living, conduct, character and actually practised human values and relations than on philosophical formulations of one's beliefs. In this regard Gandhi is more influenced by an Indian orientation that views philosophy and religion in terms of total ways of being in the world, ways of life, in which less priority is placed on intellectually or cognitively knowing the truth and more emphasis is placed on the experiential transformative realization of the truth. This may be contrasted with a dominant Western philosophical and religious orientation in which one focuses on the essential theory, belief or dogma that allows us to classify a follower as, say, a Cartesian, Kantian, Jew or Muslim. For Gandhi, as for Socrates and for dominant Indian and Asian approaches, one cannot know the good, in the fullest experiential sense of realizing the good, and do evil. For Gandhi the key to comprehending his philosophy is to focus on how he lives his life; how his values and philosophical and religious formulations are lived or embodied in his relational way of being in the world.

Even for such a remarkable human being as Gandhi, living his philosophy is not a simple task. His entire life is full of uncertainties, doubts and struggles, as he views life as a continual experiment with truth and nonviolence. As noted in the Introduction, Gandhi did not leave his followers a legacy of some philosophical, ethical, economic, political, cultural and religious blueprint. There is no Gandhi recipe for truth and nonviolence that can simply be applied to any complex contextualized situation in order to grasp a Gandhi solution. Gandhi certainly has absolute ethical and spiritual ideals and experiential claims about the nature of reality but he repeatedly formulates and reformulates his philosophical approach as he learns from his experimental successes and failures with truth and nonviolence.

In this regard Gandhi is strongly committed to his constructive work, but, just to cite the first formulation in his Constructive Programme, entitled Communal (Religious) Unity, he struggles for decades to achieve Hindu–Muslim communal harmony.[1] And during the last decade of his life, with increasing Hindu–Muslim disharmony, distrust and violence and with the Partition into India and Pakistan on religious grounds, Gandhi evaluates this constructive work as an abysmal failure. Indeed, a Hindu nationalist, who feels that Gandhi favours Muslims and betrays Hindus, assassinates him. Similarly, nothing is more emphasized in Gandhi's life than his commitment to the philosophy and practice of nonviolence. And yet late in his life, as he feels overwhelmed by the religious and political communal violence all around him, he sadly concludes that he had repeatedly miscalculated the degree to which even most of his *satyagrahis* and other nonviolent followers had ever embraced a commitment to nonviolence as a philosophy and way of life.

One of the major ways for understanding Gandhi's struggles, experiments and developing formulations and practices of truth and nonviolence can be seen in his central focus on what he calls 'Modern Civilization'. When asked by a British journalist what he thought of 'Western civilization', Gandhi famously and humorously responded: 'I think it would be a good idea.' As with most of Gandhi's humour, many layers of meaning are concealed and revealed underlying simplistic and even childlike humorous expressions. In his response about Western civilization Gandhi is engaged in dialogue and complex relations of conflicted intimacy with British colonialism. He is challenging the British hegemonic, arrogant, racist imperial claims that they are in India taking on the noble burden of bringing civilization to Indians. He is challenging colonized Indians to overcome their sense of inferiority, to stop worshipping everything British, Western and 'modern', and to be proud of what is great and morally, culturally and spiritually superior in their own civilization.

It is not always clear what Gandhi means by his frequent significant references to 'Modern Civilization' or 'Western Civilization' and to 'Ancient Civilization' or 'Indian Civilization'. Many of his perplexing and even bizarre formulations, if taken at face value, seem completely nonhistorical, unscientific, nonfactual and easily refuted. They often seem completely irrelevant to contemporary India and the world. However, if interpreted, reinterpreted and reformulated in creative ways, Gandhi's insights and expressions about civilization have profound symbolic, mythic, allegorical and even historical and scientific meaning, value and relevance.

Throughout *Hind Swaraj* and in other writings Gandhi formulates a sharp oppositional dichotomy between Modern (Western) Civilization and Ancient (Indian) Civilization. In this civilizational struggle Gandhi equates 'Modern Civilization' with the Kingdom of Satan and the God of War and 'Ancient Civilization' with the Kingdom of God and the God of Love. Typical of oppositional normative categories found in traditional myths, Gandhi's formulations attempt to abstract from particular contextual variables to reveal essential foundational truths and realities.[2]

In his Preface to the March 1910 English translation of his work Gandhi tells us that his purpose in writing *Hind Swaraj* is to show Indians that they should reject modern civilization with its violent methods and that if they would 'but revert to their own glorious civilization' they would achieve self-rule and true independence of *swaraj*. In this regard he makes many confusing assertions, such as the fact that India 'has nothing to learn from anybody else', even though Gandhi's own life and his inclusive philosophical and religious approach contradict this, and the fact that in order 'to restore India to its pristine condition, we have to return to it'.[3]

The major illustration of these latter assertions can be found in Gandhi's idealized and romanticized descriptions and evaluations of India's villages. He claims that villagers of Ancient Indian Civilization, as well as those in contemporary villages where the 'cursed modern civilization has not reached', recognize the dignity and value of manual labour. They know that cities are a 'useless encumbrance'. They know that kings and weapons are inferior to ethics, and their lawyers and doctors recognize that they are people's dependents. Common people in villages live independently and enjoy 'true Home Rule'. Traditional Indian peasants use soul-force, not brute-force or body-force, and 'have never been subdued by the sword, and never will be'. Courageous and virtuous, they know that nonviolent *Satyagraha* is the only Indian way to true *swaraj*.[4]

Similarly, Gandhi is often criticized and dismissed for his uncritical and irrelevant formulations in his chapter in *Hind Swaraj* on 'Machinery'. Attacking 'machinery' as 'the chief symbol of modern civilization' and as representing 'a great sin', Gandhi concludes that he 'cannot recall a single good point in connection with machinery'. We must never forget 'the main thing': 'It is necessary to realise that machinery is bad. We shall then be able gradually to do away with it.'[5] It is true that Gandhi later modifies and softens this view, claiming that he is not against the use of machinery or technology if it can meet real human needs and improve human life. Indeed, Gandhi himself utilizes the printing press, railroads and the mass media in spreading and implementing his philosophy. What Gandhi claims to be against is the modern 'machine craze', the worship of technology, as part of an orientation and world view that displaces meaningful labour, is dehumanizing and marginalizes ethical and spiritual priorities.

Gandhi frequently uses and develops the disease metaphor to portray Modern Western Civilization. He also emphasizes that this is not a permanent fatal condition; it is a 'curable disease' if we just return to the essential ethical and spiritual truths of Ancient Indian Civilization that alone will allow twentieth-century India to achieve true *swaraj*.[6]

What is Gandhi doing in these frequent dramatic, sweeping, judgemental formulations that usually strike contemporary readers as uncritical, romantic, bewildering and probably irrelevant for the twenty-first century? Gandhi's glorification of Indian villages, his negative attitude toward machinery and technology, and his simple disease and other negative metaphors to describe modernity seem largely irrelevant to our contemporary urban, industrial, technological, globalized world.

One can certainly understand and even identify with most of these formulations in a variety of ways using historical, anthropological, political, sociological, economic, religious and philosophical documentation and critical reflection and analysis. For example, Gandhi, despite continually professing his strong loyalty as a citizen of the British Empire, gradually becomes aware of the condescending, humiliating, judgemental attitude of the self-justifying 'civilized' British colonial rulers. Traditional Indians are viewed as inferior, backward, unethical, irrational and uncivilized. As seen in his response to the question of what he thinks about 'Western Civilization', Gandhi is intentionally providing a dramatic oppositional inversion in which he exhorts Indians to free themselves from their internalized fear, sense of inferiority, acquiescence and self-imposed enslavement and to be proud of their superior 'Ancient Civilization'. Reversing the British colonial attitude, Gandhi even tells Indians that they should feel pity for the English who are victims of an inferior, unethical, materialistic, dehumanized and meaningless 'Modern Civilization'.[7]

Even in some of Gandhi's most controversial and bewildering writings, such as those on machinery as evil or hospitals as 'institutions for propagating sin', one can recognize profound truths that seem truer today than ever. More and more people now write about what Gandhi calls the disastrous 'machine craze' that is part of a modern context of dehumanization and alienation. It expresses itself through the displacement of labour, meaninglessness, false views of progress and development, unlimited egotistic consumption, violent economic and social relations, and unsustainable relations between human beings and with nature. Similarly, more and more people now critique and provide alternatives to dominant forms of modern medicine, driven by profits and not selfless service. Millions are denied decent health care, suffer and die from preventable diseases. Modern humans become dependent on technology and drugs and don't come to terms with the underlying causes of illness or suffering, our mind–body interactions and how we perpetuate unhealthy causal conditions.[8]

Nevertheless, this critique does not minimize the fact that Gandhi's key civilizational formulations, especially in *Hind Swaraj*, are simplistic, exaggerated, uncritical, hopelessly irrelevant and simply false or nonsensical. For example, using historical, anthropological, sociological and other evidence, it would seem impossible to justify Gandhi's bold essentialized claims about Indian villages and peasants and other idealized virtues of some supposedly ethical nonviolent Ancient Indian Civilization.

Gandhi is well aware of how the actual history of India and historical institutionalized Hinduism and other religions are often extremely violent and lacking in truth, nonviolence and morality. He is aware of past violent conquests and oppressive domination, and how villages reflect considerable caste, class and patriarchal violence. He writes in later decades about how Indian villages are often dirty and unhygienic places and impose violent exploitative and oppressive relations of domination on untouchables, women, lepers and others. He clarifies that his Indian village is the village 'of my dreams'. However, key passages in *Hind Swaraj* and other writings are not so qualified and seem to be offered as actual historical accounts of what life in pre-industrial, pre-colonial India is like. Indeed, Gandhi insists that he is not presenting a 'utopian' dream but as a pragmatic idealist he is presenting views of an India that once existed and that is now practically achievable.[9]

If one does not simply dismiss Gandhi's controversial assertions and judgements about Modern Western Civilization and Ancient Indian Civilization, there are two related ways of rendering such formulations insightful, significant and relevant for the contemporary world. First, one could approach such oppositional civilizational accounts not on the level of literal, historical and scientific descriptions and judgements, but rather as highly symbolic, mythic, allegorical, literary and aesthetic formulations consistent with Gandhi's interpretive insights. Second, one could approach such oppositional accounts as essentialized formulations of two ways of being in the world, two civilizational narratives, two paradigms that attempt to uncover the essential values, priorities and modes of being abstracted from the complex, particular, historical and cultural variables that appear in any ancient or modern context.

Instructive for approaching the ancient and modern civilizational formulations is Gandhi's famous and controversial approach to the *Bhagavad-Gita*. This is especially significant since the *Gita* is Gandhi's favourite ethical and spiritual text and his guide for how to live a most developed, exemplary human life. The *Gita* provides Gandhi with his favourite path of *karma yoga* of renunciation in action: act, based on self-knowledge and fulfilling your *dharma* or duty, with an attitude of nonattachment to the results of your action. What astonishes others is Gandhi's startling claim that the *Gita* should be read, interpreted and applied as a 'Gospel of Nonviolence'.[10]

After all, the dramatic setting of the *Gita* is the battlefield, with the two sides about to engage in unavoidable warfare. Krishna instructs the great warrior Arjuna, leader of the Pandavas, that he should engage in the war, acting on knowledge of his personal *karma* and *karmic* situation and fulfilling his duty as a leader of the *Khastriya* or warrior caste, but he should renounce any ego-attachment to the results of his action. As the best-known Hindu scripture the *Gita* has been the source for numerous influential interpretations and commentaries. These include those by Shankara and other ancient philosophers, up through the major nationalist interpretations during the anti-colonial independence struggles, and continuing to the present day with many diverse interpretations. In addition, hundreds of millions of Indians have embraced versions and interpretations of the *Gita* through rituals, art, literature and other cultural creations, and the *Gita*'s influence continues through contemporary expressions of popular culture. It does not seem to have occurred to the great philosophers and other interpreters or to the masses of devotees that the essential message of the *Gita* is nonviolence. In fact some scholars describe Gandhi's seemingly bizarre interpretation as a hermeneutic disaster. They claim that his approach may have fictional value or it may be how he subjectively reframes the text to fit in with his own philosophy of nonviolence, but this has nothing to do with a serious, rigorous interpretation of the actual text.

Gandhi's well-known response is that the *Gita* should not be read in a literal or historical way, as if it is describing an actual historical battle or is literally instructing Arjuna to fight. It should be read as a highly symbolic allegory. The battlefield is an effective allegorical device for portraying the battle that goes on within each of us, the battle between darkness and light, our lower and higher nature, untruth and truth, violence and nonviolence. Even more instructive and relevant to Gandhi's civilizational formulations are his insightful hermeneutic reflections on how he interprets the *Gita* or any other significant text. Every reading is always a rereading, every interpretation a reinterpretation, every formulation a reformulation. We are always engaged in a complex, dynamic process of the interpretation of meaning. The ancient Indians who first formulate the *Gita* over 2,000 years ago exist within their own horizons of meaning shaped by their historical, social, economic, cultural, political, religious and linguistic variables. Human beings today live in very different horizons of meaning shaped by all kinds of developments, including past interpretations of the *Gita* and major contemporary variables. In this sense, how we relate to the text, what messages or voices are heard and which are marginalized or silenced, what is significant or insignificant, relevant or irrelevant, and what the *Gita* means to us is part of a dynamic creative process of reconstitution and reinterpretation. In this sense there are multiple *Gitas* or, expressed differently, the text is not fixed and closed but it is always a part of an open-ended process of multiple rereadings, reinterpretations and reformulations.

In his approach Gandhi claims that the ancient Indian *rishi*s or seers, mystics and other enlightened beings were extraordinary human beings who had intuitions and insights into ethical and spiritual truths that speak to us in the most profound ways today. However, ancient Indians who formulated and interpreted the *Gita* were also limited human beings who used limited linguistic formulations consistent with their limited historical and cultural horizons. Therefore Gandhi is not claiming that ancient Indians expressed a Gandhian commitment to nonviolence. Similarly, Gandhi realizes that the Indian nationalists, who offer interpretations of the *Gita* as an invaluable text in the struggle for national independence, often emphasize how it justifies the use of violence for their worthy cause.

For Gandhi the *Bhagavad-Gita* is a gospel of nonviolence because that is how we can read it as its most developed, ethical, spiritual and urgently needed message today. Parts of the text, as with all scriptures and other significant writings, may strike us as irrational, immoral, untruthful and violent, and we should revise or simply reject such passages. Although not read as a gospel of nonviolence by earlier Indians, that is the text's purest and most developed message for us today. This does not mean that anything goes, and we can subjectively read, interpret and apply the *Gita* any way that pleases us. The text is not infinitely malleable; it has basic structures, symbolic expressions, key principles and teachings. Some readings are misreadings or are of limited explanatory value and limited ethical and spiritual significance. However, reading and interpreting the essential meaning of the *Gita* as a gospel of nonviolence is an interpretation that is consistent with the essential textual values and teachings and is the most developed, creative, significant and relevant rendering of the open-ended text for us today.

If one applies this hermeneutic approach to Gandhi's seemingly uncritical, unhistorical, idyllic formulations of 'Ancient Civilization', then he is not claiming that he is offering factual or accurate descriptions of how premodern Indians actually live. They often support human relations that express economic, political, military, gendered, caste-based and other forms of violence and untruth. They often violate the true social and ethical sense of *dharma* or moral obligation and do not experience deeper senses of reality. What Gandhi is claiming is that there are basic intuitions, values, principles and experiential realizations that define 'Ancient Civilization' at its highest ethical and spiritual levels. We can develop those essential Indian contributions to higher levels of ethical and spiritual realization that relate significantly to our contemporary world.[11]

Consistent with this approach, one can interpret the meaning of Gandhi's formulations on 'Ancient Civilization' and improve on them. This involves rejecting what is hopelessly uncritical and irrelevant and reinterpreting and reformulating what is essential in new creative ways that are significant today.

Similarly, many of Gandhi's formulations of 'Modern Civilization', with their absolute, unqualified negative descriptions and judgemental dismissals, should not be read and interpreted simply as accurate factual claims. Gandhi himself is influenced by many modern writings in their critiques of premodern orientations, and in their contributions to his thinking about individual autonomy, freedom, equality, democracy and other values. What Gandhi claims is that there are basic intuitions, values, principles and experiential realizations that define dominant formulations of 'Modern Civilization' and that most shape our views of success, progress, development and civilization. These dominant essential human relations trap us in illusory causal cycles of untruth and multidimensional violence that define how we relate to our self, to other humans and other sentient beings, and to nature. They are obstacles to developing our ethical and spiritual potential for dealing with our crises today.

At the same time, in a dynamic, open-ended approach, Gandhi and we today can develop essential contributions found in modern writings to higher levels of realization. We can reinterpret and reformulate more adequate meanings of self-rule and self-realization, true individual autonomy, real freedom and equality, deeper democracy and independence and interdependence, and the proper relations of humans to technology and to nature in ways that relate most significantly to our contemporary world.

Such an approach to Gandhi's civilizational account reveals the value, but also the limitations, of a frequent interpretation of Gandhi and his philosophy as premodern, or modern or postmodern. In his positive valuation of 'Ancient Civilization' and his usual critique of and hostility toward modernity, it is tempting simply to classify Gandhi as an engaged premodern thinker and practitioner. This is what many devotees and most critics do. However, this ignores Gandhi's radical critique of traditional hierarchical India, with its fixed relational violent structures of domination, and how Gandhi's complex philosophy, religion and cultural practices are not simply traditional or premodern.

A smaller number of interpreters have claimed that, on a deeper level, getting beyond Gandhi's external appearance, idiosyncratic practices and premodern expressions, he is essentially modern. However, this ignores how even when Gandhi is using such seemingly modern Western concepts as individual autonomy, self-reliance, individual rights and freedoms, democracy, and independence, he is reinterpreting, reformulating and reapplying them in ways that critique dominant features of 'Modern Civilization'.

It has become fashionable among some interpreters in recent decades to classify Gandhi as postmodern, especially in his critique of Western hegemonic universalizing of modern violent philosophies and practices. These postmodernist interpreters focus on Gandhi's insistence on pluralism, diversity, respect for differences, multiple perspectives and narratives, and the need to situate and contextualize each approach as expressing relative limited truths.[12] Although this classification seems to make Gandhi relevant in bringing him in line with key European postmodernist thinkers and some other recent Western philosophical developments, it ignores essential premodern and also modern influences on Gandhi's philosophy and practices. Such an interpretation of Gandhi as postmodernist ignores or devalues his significant claims about the truth of our fundamental oneness or unity, with a respect for differences, his endorsement of absolute regulative ideals and his powerful critique of and resistance to perspectives not based on truth and nonviolence.

Although the premodern–modern–postmodern categorizations have some interpretive and explanatory value, this classification is inadequate for grasping Gandhi's philosophy and practices and how they can be reinterpreted and reformulated as relevant and significant for our contemporary world. When Gandhi brings his experiences, readings and diverse expressions of what he sometimes labels as 'Ancient Civilization' and 'Modern Civilization' into a dynamic relation, what emerges is a new civilizational model of how to conduct ourselves meaningfully. When Gandhi, through his experiments with truth, brings into dynamic relation the premodern, the modern and the postmodern world outlooks and orientations, key positive and negative relational values in each approach interact with the other approaches. What emerges in Gandhi's innovative philosophy and practices is something radically new that cannot be subsumed under the inadequate tripartite classification.

Most significant for our contemporary world, Gandhi's broad, essentialized, judgemental and often seemingly uncritical formulations of 'Ancient Civilization' and 'Modern Civilization' are his attempt at uncovering two radically different human ways of being in the world. Abstracting from the diverse historical and cultural variables that appear in all ancient and modern contexts and shape all ancient and modern texts, Gandhi formulates two essential civilizational narratives revealing two oppositional paradigms. These two accounts of our human mode of being in the world reveal contrasting approaches to the nature of reality with radically different values and priorities. Gandhi is especially concerned with critiquing and resisting 'Modern Civilization', an orientation that defines modern Western industrialized, technological, globalized relations today. This dominant modern philosophy and its practices are untruthful, violent and leading humankind and the planet earth towards disaster.

Very briefly formulated, Gandhi submits that dominant characteristics of 'Modern Civilization' express economic, political,

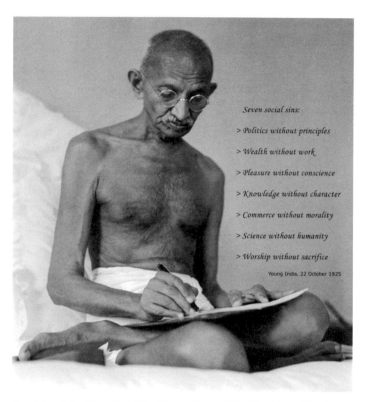

Seven social sins:

> Politics without principles

> Wealth without work

> Pleasure without conscience

> Knowledge without character

> Commerce without morality

> Science without humanity

> Worship without sacrifice

Young India, 22 October 1925

Gandhi made the 'Seven Social Sins' famous for providing his critique of 'modern civilization'.

cultural, psychological and other forms of violence, and 'moderns' are socialized and rewarded in ways that perpetuate the systemic structural violence of the status quo. 'Modern Civilization' privileges the illusory modern, separate, 'independent' self, with its aggressive, ego-defined, endless desires, needs and attachments. It privileges individual, social, national and other differences. 'Modern Civilization' thus contributes to modern experiments with untruth. In its basic assumptions, approaches and world view, it violates the fundamental ethical and ontological nature of nonviolent interconnected unifying truth and reality and results in diverse dangerous forms of violent civilizational disharmony.

According to Gandhi, human beings have a duty to provide the means to satisfy the material needs of impoverished and suffering human beings, but 'Modern Civilization' is violently and untruthfully materialistic in that it emphasizes the material in a radically reductionistic manner. Modern approaches organize life around endless insatiable material production and consumption. They conceptualize models of development, progress, success, happiness and standard of living in terms of maximizing levels of material production and consumption. In this way they emphasize bodily desires, with the proliferation of endless needs and wants. According to Gandhi they even do a poor job of fulfilling such bodily desires, since they lack the necessary qualities and virtues of self-discipline and self-rule over desires. Indeed, when egocentric bodily desires are so emphasized and detached from the total, body–mind–spirit, integral human being, they represent our lowest base 'animalistic' nature and provide the least adequate criteria for human conduct and civilization.

Here one finds Gandhi's critique of the modern 'machine craze' as a major part of materialist, consumerist, violent and untruthful ways of being in the world. Such a machine-centric and money-centric orientation privileges and worships the idols of technology and does not express the moral and social relations of limited appropriate technology. It produces and expresses the alienation of labour and dehumanizing and violent human relations of growing inequality. It marginalizes any deep sense of morality and duty that is at the heart of a human-centric approach to our real ethical and spiritual development.

Gandhi's critique of 'Modern Civilization' raises insightful contributions that can be related to earlier Western writings critical of the modern, post-Enlightenment dominant tradition. Some of these dissenters, such as Tolstoy, Ruskin and Thoreau, deeply influence Gandhi. Gandhi's critique can also be related to some modern ethical thinkers, as evidenced in Kant's formulation of the Categorical Imperative to treat others as ends and never merely as means, and even more so in Marx's analysis of alienated labour in his 'Manuscripts of 1844' and formulations in his later writings.

Gandhi's critique can also be related to approaches of theologians such as Paul Tillich, existential dialogic philosophers such as Martin Buber in his ethical and spiritual I–Thou relational analysis, much of twentieth-century existentialist philosophy and literature, and recent approaches to our ecological crisis and the unsustainability of dominant economic and environmental models of development.

Gandhi is not claiming that modern individual human beings, social relations, cultures and civilizations begin the exploitation and destruction of other humans, other sentient beings and nature. Ancient and later premodern human beings certainly live unethical and untruthful lives that often express class, caste, misogynist and other forms of violence. Values, relations and structures expressing alienation, destructive conflict, ignorance and immorality are obstacles to ethical and spiritual development and limit these premodern human beings and cultures.

What Gandhi is claiming, as seen in his abstract essentialist formulations of 'Modern Civilization', is that dominant modernity introduces and promotes a modern paradigm that is qualitatively and quantitatively new, dehumanizing, alienating and destructive. It expresses relations that are self-destructive and destructive of other beings and of nature. The new models of human and civilizational progress and development dominate the modern world and entrap us in vicious causal cycles of untruth, violence, disharmony, conflict, war and unsustainability.

In dominant forms of 'Modern Civilization', modern developed humans are separate, egoistic, 'autonomous' individuals who are able to use instrumental reason to calculate whatever means are necessary to further their economic, political and other self-interested ends. It is not as if modernity introduces the philosophical and theological ideas that humans are special and superior and that nature exists in order to be subdued and exploited as a means to higher human or divine ends. However, modernity introduces new values, analyses and rationales for such exploitation and domination. Adopting the Baconian approach to scientific method and knowledge, nature is the objective valueless material means enabling humans to achieve control and domination. And when human beings later achieve the marriage of science and technology with the promotion of the 'machine craze', there is an unprecedented explosion in the capacity of modern humans and civilizations to maximize priorities of material production and consumption and to pursue objectives of maximizing power and domination over other humans and cultures, nature and all life on the planet.

Gandhi examines how the dominant forms that this modern paradigm of self, human relations, civilization, development and progress take are defined by the development of capitalism, industrialization, urbanization and globalization. Increasingly all of life becomes commodified and capitalized. Objectified nature and objectified human beings are conceived as commodities. Those who exploit their asymmetrical power relations treat commodified humans and nature as means for maximizing profit, control and domination. For Gandhi, this dominant model destroys the dignity of human labour, the moral and spiritual value of each human being and of nature and is economically and ecologically unsustainable. Such a dominant modern paradigm, with its philosophies and practices, poses the most dangerous obstacle to realizing basic nonviolent and truthful relations of integrity, harmony and real human and civilizational development, standard of living and progress.[13]

Rather than literal or historical descriptions, Gandhi's formulations of superior 'Ancient Civilization' are primarily intended to challenge us to rethink civilizational assumptions, values and relations. Gandhi's 'Ancient Civilization' emphasizes a paradigm and orientation that is human-centric rather than machine-centric and money-centric, is essentially nonviolent, emphasizes morality and spiritual realization, addresses our higher human capacities and focuses on human integrity and harmonious relations with other beings and with nature.

In his formulations of 'Ancient Civilization' Gandhi is selectively focusing on remarkable ethical and spiritual, nonviolent and truthful intuitions and experiential realizations, found in the ancient texts but also accessible to all human beings and cultures and constitutive of developed human realization in later premodern, modern and contemporary life. Gandhi, the philosophical and practical realist and pragmatist, is not recommending an unrealistic romantic utopian path of returning to some ancient Indian mode of being. His formulations are rendered most significant and relevant if we interpret them as emphasizing that we must return to the ancient texts as valuable resources for uncovering ethical and spiritual insights, in order to reappropriate and reformulate them, selectively and critically, in new contextual and civilizational ways that speak to the crises of the contemporary world.

Gandhi's civilizational paradigms, with their contrasting philosophies and practices, provide the interpretative framework for analysing his insightful analysis of religion.[14] As seen in previous chapters Gandhi frequently identifies himself and his approach as religious or spiritual and more specifically as Hindu, but his formulations often seem uncritical and inconsistent. Much of this confusion arises from the fact that Gandhi's approach to religion is so dynamic, open-ended, critical and self-critical, tolerant and respectful in affirming the unity and equality of diverse religious paths. Gandhi may be viewed by some as deeply religious but not in any exclusive, traditional or institutionalized sense of religion.

In some passages Gandhi prefers language with no 'God' references; in others he focuses on truth rather than God, as in his 'Truth is God' preferred formulations; and in others he emphasizes devotion to a personal God. In some of the latter passages, in which Gandhi tells us that he leaves everything to God and in which God speaks to him in unexpected ways, Gandhi's approach seems baffling, irrational, immoral, superstitious and even dangerous. These confusing formulations seem at odds with Gandhi's philosophy and his usual approach to religion.

Much of this confusion can be removed by emphasizing a key distinction in Gandhi's philosophy, consistent with his civilizational and other analysis, between ideal, absolute, universal, essential, true religion ('Religion') and actual, relative, historical, organized, institutionalized religion ('religion') and religions ('religions'). Relative religion and religions include specific scriptures and other texts, authoritative leaders and structural hierarchies, rituals and other practices, and other limited contextualized expressions.

Gandhi refers to ideal Religion when he asserts that Hinduism and all other religions express nonviolence and that all religions are diverse paths to the one, spiritual, Absolute Truth and Ultimate Reality. He is offering a description of actual contextualized religion, religions and religious life when he repeatedly asserts that religion consists of nonviolence, love, compassion, selfless service, peace-making, tolerance and mutual respect. Gandhi is not providing a philosophy and approach to Religion based simply on his imaginary construction of absolute ideals. He claims to have experiences of the eternal and permanent Absolute Religion. That is why he is certain that it is real. But just as Gandhi asserts that no one knows non-violence and no one knows truth, no one fully knows Religion. Gandhi has occasional, imperfect, temporary 'glimpses' of Religion. One of the greatest dangers, as evidenced throughout the history of religions, is to regard your imperfect religion as possessing the exclusive absolute reality, thus making into absolute truth what is relative. Other religions are then regarded as essentially false, sinful, evil and dangerous, thus providing a false justification for relating to others with intolerance, disrespect, hatred, violence and war.

As with economic, political, cultural and other civilizational relations as ways of being in the world, religious people are at best moving from one relative truth to greater relative truth; from one relative religious perspective to a greater relative religious perspective, more nonviolent, more truthful and closer to Religion as the essential ideal.

In Gandhi's approach all religions contain significant ethical and spiritual insights and contributions but they also contain impurities, multidimensional and structural violence and untruths. They express human limitations reflecting the relative relational situatedness of past and present historical and cultural contexts. Believers should not be shamed or overwhelmed by aggressive proponents of other religions or of anti-religious 'Modern Civilization'. Believers should be free to think critically and to act freely and with integrity consistent with their own deepest experiences. This includes being free to reject what is experienced in their own religion as immoral, untruthful or no longer relevant. They should be free to purify and develop their own religion. This includes being free to accept religious insights and contributions from other religions as means for developing the ethical and spiritual depth, significance and relevance of one's own religious life.

This approach to culture and religion, with the need for intercultural and interreligious dialogue, is expressed in Gandhi's frequently cited formulation: 'I do not want my house to be walled in on all sides and my windows to be stuffed. I want the cultures of all lands to be blown about my house as freely as possible.' As Gandhi concludes: 'Mine is not a religion of the prison-house.'[15]

Here one finds Gandhi's approach to religion and religions in terms of dynamic, open-ended, developmental, interreligious and intercultural dialogue with the need for empathy, tolerance, respect and mutual understanding. This approach is grounded in Gandhi's philosophy with the key Absolute Religion–relative religion distinction providing the basis for his fundamental conviction upholding the interconnected, interrelated unity and equality of all religions as diverse paths to the same truth and reality. Gandhi goes beyond the usual political rationales in some secular forms of 'Modern Civilization' for pluralism, tolerance and the right of individuals to be free to practise their own religion. Based on his ethical and spiritual philosophy of *satya* and *ahimsa*, with formulations of Religion and religion, Gandhi provides a religious justification for tolerance, mutual respect and mutual understanding. These provide the means by which religious believers become more religious, religions become purified and develop ethically and spiritually, and religious believers move closer to ideal Religion, closer to realizing nonviolence, truth and reality.

This approach to religion is expressed in Gandhi's challenging approach to religious scriptures, as seen in the earlier formulation of his interpretation of the *Bhagavad-Gita* as a gospel on non-violence. Gandhi's hermeneutic reflections arise from his engagement with the troubling status and functioning of religious scriptures in his life, in history and in his world.[16] He finds that Hinduism, Christianity, Islam and other organized and institutionalized religions often use scriptures as the basis for class and caste exploitation, oppression of women and others, justification of violence and war, and, in short, for what Gandhi analyses as ethical and spiritual untruths. Religions often assert that their scriptures are not to be questioned since they are the word of God. And such uncritical acceptance of scriptures is enforced, often with severe punishments for those raising questions of interpretation and justification. In this regard Gandhi is very critical of traditional religions, and he often makes orthodox religious authorities, including those with political and economic power, very uncomfortable.

How does Gandhi deal with orthodox religious claims that their scriptures justify and necessitate, say, the brutal violent punishment, even death, of women, nonbelievers and others who violate the divine norms and injunctions? Gandhi affirms his faith that scriptures do contain profound insights into ideal, absolute, universal, ethical and spiritual truths. However, religious truths expressed in religion, including those in scriptures, are always transmitted through and formulated by imperfect human beings. That is why scriptural formulations have to be situated in their specific, human, historical, social and cultural contexts in order to comprehend the expression and meaning of specific language, symbolism, mythic and ritual formulations, ethical teachings and social codes. Since those human transmitters and expressers are not perfect, their scriptural expressions are always imperfect, falling short of the ideals of nonviolence, truth and religion.

In some dramatic illustrations Gandhi is told that certain scriptural claims necessitate chopping off limbs of sinners, stoning to death and other cruel executions, sacrifice of animals, holy wars against infidels and other acts that he finds violate ideals of truth and nonviolence. Gandhi asserts that if the Bible, the Qur'an or any other scripture does in fact contradict human reason and authentic human experience, then you should reject what the scripture tells you to do.

Since all scriptures contain relative truths, with impurities and imperfections and untruths, they should be interpreted as limited attempts at realizing more perfect ideals. Each scripture represents a different relative orientation and path, or multiple paths, grounded in and reflecting particular linguistic, social, cultural and other contexts. That is why no scripture contains an absolute exclusive truth, why we should be tolerant and respect other scriptural paths and why we can learn from other scriptural revelations.[17]

What this means today for Gandhi's hermeneutic project is that those believers who accept certain foundational scriptures should identify with and appropriate deep essential truths revealed in their scriptures, but they must also critically question and purify and develop their own scriptural relations and understandings. A scripture, in this sense, is not something static and closed. Rather it is a defining, often foundational, part of an ongoing process in which we provide new, more adequate ethical and spiritual interpretations and formulations in terms of our evolving, contextually related, developmental understanding.

Gandhi offers a valuable approach to religion today with his absolute–relative distinctions, oppositional civilizational formulations and call for a new paradigm that reappropriates what is of value from the past as integrated with other contributions in ways that are contextually sensitive and relevant. With so much destructive religious violence, war and untruth in the world, religion seems to be more of the problem than the solution when dealing with religious, cultural, economic, political, scientific, technological and environmental crises. Gandhi's attempt at offering a new paradigm of religion, with its commitment to nonviolence and truth, to ethically and ontologically unifying harmonious relations, to intrareligious and interreligious dialogue and unity with a respect for differences, has great explanatory value and transformative potential.

Gandhi's philosophical framework, including his approach to religion, is often difficult to apply and gives rise to many legitimate questions and concerns. There is no simple Gandhi blueprint that we can simply apply to overcome religious conflicts, multidimensional and structural violence and untruths. Gandhi repeatedly experiences questions and concerns in his own experiments with truth relating to religion, other religions and even Hinduism, experiments that he often assesses as failures.

How can Gandhi justify his foundational claim that he experiences, albeit imperfectly, the Absolute Truth of Religion? How can Gandhi justify his foundational descriptions and judgments about the integral, dynamic relations between the Absolute Religion and relative religion and religions? What about other religious believers who claim that they experience the Absolute Truth of Religion, and their God or Ultimate Reality contradicts Gandhi's philosophical ideal? They reject Gandhi's ethical and ontological framework and approach. Their true Religion does not include an essential Gandhi version of nonviolence and rejects Gandhi's formulations of truth as expressions of untruth. They reject Gandhi's powerful image of religions as expressing different legitimate paths for ascending and reaching the same top of the mountain. For them, other religions are taking false paths and will never reach the top of the mountain or, put differently, other religions are not even on the one true mountain. In addition, what about contemporary cultural relativists who reject the adoption of all universal essential absolutes, even Gandhi's more inclusive and tolerant absolutes, as epistemologically inadequate, intersubjectively unverifiable, hegemonic and even multidimensionally violent?

What this means is that Gandhi's remarkable ethical and spiritual approach, with his commitment to a new paradigm grounded in ideals of truth and nonviolence, his civilizational accounts and his analysis of religion has tremendous explanatory value and trans-formative potential for addressing crises in the contemporary world. But Gandhi does not have simple answers or all of the answers. His approach to civilization, including religion, emphasizes empathy, tolerance, mutual respect and mutual understanding, but it also involves active critical transformative engagement. As in other situations involving great violence and untruth, the appro-priate Gandhi approach to much of civilizational and religious violence, war and untruth in the world includes *satyagraha*, determined nonviolent noncooperation and active resistance. It also includes economic, cultural, educational and religious constructive work that is essential for the morally and spiritually transformative process toward greater nonviolence and truth.

8

Gandhi Today

Is there some valuable Gandhi legacy for the twenty-first century? Do his philosophy and practices have significant meaning and relevance today? As has been noted throughout this book, Gandhi was widely admired but also controversial during his lifetime, and he remains so today. There is no need to repeat all of the analysis and conclusions in earlier chapters that indicate Gandhi's possible relevance and significance in terms of his philosophy and practices regarding violence and nonviolence, truth, morality, economics and politics, religion, class and caste, gender and other oppression, freedom and equality, environmental destruction, and other major topics today. We'll focus on a few of the key contributions in Gandhi's philosophical legacy for the contemporary world.

Some of the Gandhi controversies, which continue to generate heated debate, relate to Gandhi's life, individual practices and personal idiosyncrasies. Here one finds such controversies as those arising from some of Gandhi's assertions and practices regarding sexual desires, *brahmacharya* or celibacy, women and gender relations, birth control and rape; his relations with his wife Kasturba and his four sons, especially the tragic life of his son Harilal; and his medical cures, diets and fasts.

Some of the continuing controversies relate to Gandhi's general philosophical, moral, economic, political, cultural, religious and educational views and practices. Here one finds such controversies as those arising from his claims about progress, technology and

A studio photograph of Gandhi taken in London at the request of Lord Irwin in 1931.

'Modern Civilization'; his approach to contemporary multi-dimensional and structural violence, including today's religious violence, terrorism and war; and whether the application of his approach to politics, economics, education, development, industrialization, globalization, independence and freedom today is reactionary and completely irrelevant.

Even in India today there are four large groupings of Indians who strongly oppose Gandhi and Gandhian approaches. First, there are *Hindutva* ('Hinduness', a word probably coined by Gandhi's opponent V. D. Savarkar) Hindus, who tend to be rightwing nationalists, claiming that true India is a Hindu nation. A Savarkar follower and *Hindutva* ideologue, Nathuram Godse, assassinated Gandhi. *Hindutva* proponents often charge that Gandhi favoured Muslims and other minorities over Hindus, was responsible for the India–Pakistan Partition and for the Kashmir crisis, and made Hindus and India weak by insisting on nonviolence. *Hindutva* political parties and movements remain strong in various parts of India, and an alliance led by the Bharatiya Janata Party ('Indian People's Party'), often expressing strong *Hindutva* values, was the ruling party in India from 1998 to 2004.

Gandhi certainly sympathizes with the backlash expressed by *Hindutva* proponents against the insults, humiliation and oppression directed at India in general and at Hinduism in particular. However, he is strongly critical of Hindutva's approach to Indian nationalism, religion, violence and militarism, and its fundamental dichotomous orientation of Hindu self versus non-Hindu other.

Second, there are *dalits*, the most oppressed and downtrodden, perhaps numbering 250 million. As was seen, Gandhi calls these 'untouchables' or 'outcastes' *Harijans* ('Children of God'). Anti-Gandhi *dalits*, usually Ambedkarites, charge that Gandhi really favours an oppressive, hierarchical, caste-based Hinduism, even if he claims to oppose the practice of untouchability. They charge that Gandhi was paternalistically disempowering in his approach, claiming that he could represent untouchable voices; that in focusing on the voluntary change of caste-privileged Hindus, he in fact allows for the continuation of the violent, caste-based status quo; and that he refuses to unequivocally reject the Hindu caste system.

In defence of Gandhi one can submit that his philosophy and practices are essentially anti-caste; that beneath some idealized caste formulations and pragmatic contextualized reasons for compromising and not wanting to alienate caste Hindus, Gandhi himself is against caste. This is evidenced in his ashram practices, promotion of intercaste marriages and willingness to sacrifice his life for the cause. Even today the overwhelming majority of untouchables retain a very positive view of Mahatma Gandhi. Antagonists focus on and exacerbate differences and overlook how much even Ambedkar and Gandhi have in common. One can reformulate a Gandhian philosophy, consistent with his principles and practices, that now emphasizes the need to eliminate caste.

Third, there are the Naxalites, an informal name that refers to various revolutionary communist groups and is taken from a peasant uprising in the West Bengal town of Naxalbari in 1967. Usually classified as Maoist and described by Prime Minister Manmohan Singh as the biggest internal threat to India, military and other government reports in 2010 claim that Naxalites are very active in at least thirteen states and have increasing control over about one-third of India. Fuelled by reaction against the exploitation of peasants and tribals, the Naxal movement appeals to millions of impoverished, oppressed, suffering Indians, who are part of the 'other India' and not beneficiaries of 'modern India'. These impoverished and exploited Indians are victims of the growing class inequalities, lack of real development, government corruption and repressive police and other forms of violence.

Gandhi certainly shares a lot with the Naxalites in their moral commitments, sense of injustice and identification with the needs of the most disadvantaged, as seen in their selfless service, sacrifice and willingness to die. However, Gandhi rejects their ruthlessness, violence, terror, armed insurrection and their view that their ends justify any means.

Fourth, there are 'modern' Indians, the most influential and powerful grouping, who have become very successful and privileged economically, politically and socially. Perhaps 400 million Indians have in a short period of time developed a new sense of self-confidence in their rising standard of living and in the future of a superpower India. For most of them Gandhi is simply irrelevant when it comes to their values, world view and ways of living. However, to some of them, Gandhi's example and his powerful message are an annoyance and at times a threat to their personal priorities and to India's rising economic, political and military power.

'Modern Indians', who often express admiration for the sacrifices and ideals of Mahatma Gandhi, correctly recognize that Gandhi is very critical of their modern India of ego-driven materialism and consumerism, with the exploitation of human and natural resources and with an anti-Gandhian view of standard of living and progress. Gandhi's extensive critique of 'Modern Civilization', as analysed in the previous chapter, applies to these 'modern' Indians.

What has been said about admiration for Gandhi, controversies and anti-Gandhi values, priorities and policies in India is mirrored throughout the contemporary world. For example, the fastest growing religions and religious forces throughout the world express diverse contextualized reactions against the values and effects of dominant modern Western civilization. Such religious forces usually express a very anti-Gandhi orientation. This is seen in their religious justifications of war and violence, of hierarchical privilege and power, of religiously defined states and violent legal systems and of the oppression of women and minorities. Perhaps the greatest contrast with Gandhi's philosophy of truth and nonviolence can be seen in how these religious forces embrace their fundamental classifications of the nonbelieving 'other' as essentially different, as evil and as an object of intolerance, unworthy of respect and justifying severe multidimensional and structural violence.

The most pervasive and dominant illustration of anti-Gandhi values as the 'modern' way of being in the contemporary world can be seen in how Western industrial civilization provides the model for transnational corporations and globalization, for the military-industrial complex and the modern state, and for assessing development, progress and success or failure in China, South Korea, Brazil, the United Kingdom, the United States and other nations. In such a modern world, admiration for Gandhi may at times seem like admiring some premodern relic in a museum.

Such a presentation of Gandhi's legacy as largely irrelevant offers a one-sided and false picture, not only with regard to his continuing influence during the past six decades, but especially with regard to the present and future significance of his philosophy and practices in addressing the most pressing contemporary crises. There are, of course, millions of human beings who acknowledge their indebtedness to Gandhi's exemplary role model, philosophy and practices. This is most obvious in the tributes paid to Gandhi by numerous political, moral and spiritual leaders, including Nobel Peace Prize recipients. A very limited sampling of such well-known leaders, who acknowledge their indebtedness to Gandhi or are identified as Gandhian figures, includes Martin Luther King Jr, César Chávez, Lanza del Vasto, Nelson Mandela, Desmond Tutu, the Dalai Lama, Vaclav Havel, Thich Nhat Hanh and Aung San Suu Kyi.

This indebtedness to and identification with Gandhi and his legacy is also apparent in the frequent documentation of Gandhi-inspired nonviolent resistance and liberation movements throughout Asia, Africa, Central and South America, North America and Europe. A very small sampling includes many human rights and pro-democracy struggles, antiwar and peace activism, campaigns for nuclear disarmament, environmental movements, the u.s. civil rights movement, the Polish Solidarity movement, the Czech Velvet Revolution, the overthrow of Marcos in the Philippines, the School of the Americas Watch and numerous nonviolent resistance movements in Latin America.

What is often overlooked, and is even more consistent with Gandhi's philosophy and practices, are the millions of unrecognized 'ordinary' human beings, really extraordinary human beings, who are part of Gandhi's powerful legacy. In so many diverse, admirable ways they embrace Gandhi values in their personal lives and actions, their ways of relating to others and to nature, their noncooperation and nonviolent resistance to dominant violent modern economic, political and military policies, and their experiments with alternative ways of being in the world through nonviolent and truthful constructive work.

What may be most significant in assessing Gandhi's legacy is the profound influence, often unacknowledged and usually unexpected, that Gandhi has had on policymakers, ordinary citizens and major historical developments. For cynics or so-called 'realists' it may be tempting to dismiss such influences as mere lip service, hypocrisy or utopian dreaming unrelated to actual practice, but they would be only partially correct and would sometimes be out of touch with reality.

Four remarkable illustrations from India of such profound, unexpected and usually unacknowledged Gandhi influence, may be cited. This small sample of major Gandhi influences from India is also significant in its relevant lessons dealing with contemporary crises in other nations and in our globally interconnected world.

First, for several decades after independence, scholars and others wrote numerous pieces on why 'India' as a modern, democratic nation state was an impossible experiment. With its extreme poverty, illiteracy, overpopulation and underdevelopment, with its extreme divisions based on regional, linguistic, communal, caste and religious identities, and with its lack of modern unifying historical and cultural forces of nationalism, the artificially constructed 'India' was destined to either fall apart or barely survive as a failed state. Remarkably, even acknowledging its violence, corruption, poverty, secessionist movements, human rights violations and other unresolved crises and weaknesses, India has survived, developed and even flourished as a vibrant, modern, democratic nation. For many this has been nothing short of 'miraculous', especially considering India's daunting challenges and when comparing modern India with its neighbours and with numerous 'failed' African and other nations throughout the world.

What should be appreciated is the profound influence Gandhi's example and his continuing legacy play in modern India. Here one finds a Gandhi legacy with his emphasis on inclusivism, tolerance, mutual respect, freedom and equality, democratic empowerment, civilizational harmony, nonviolent relations, duty and rights, openended experiments with truth and new ways of living. Here one also finds Gandhi's pride in India's ethical and cultural past and his confidence in its unlimited future and even in its vital contributions toward global harmony and civilizational development.

Second, after several decades of growing non-Gandhian and anti-Gandhian developments among those with power and privilege, there has been a remarkable renewed interest in Gandhi and his legacy in the twenty-first century. In numerous ways a profound Gandhi influence is having effects in the concerns, thinking and policies of modern India, even among a significant minority of highly educated and powerful Indian elite. And even much more significant is the potential influence of integrating Gandhi's insights, contributions and legacy as a vital part of new, urgently needed approaches for dealing with present and future crises.

In this regard one finds an increasing serious openness to Gandhi and his legacy on the part of economic and political leaders, experts on terrorism and security, educators, environmentalists, scientists and engineers. Here one finds recent writings on such topics as Gandhian economics and management, Gandhian engineering, Gandhian education, Gandhian ecology and Gandhian inclusive democracy. An increasing number of outstanding scientists and other experts are fully aware that their dominant modern models, approaches and priorities may have contributed to short-term material and other gains for many but are now economically and environmental unsustainable. Even if focusing only on global climate change or some other particular threat to human life and the planet, experts increasingly recognize the need for new paradigms with new ways of assessing success, standard of living, progress, happiness, self-realization and fulfilment. In this regard Gandhi is often the catalyst for allowing modern human beings to rethink our inadequate and dangerous world view. This is increasingly true not only in India but also in the West and throughout the world.

An important illustration of this Gandhi influence with policymakers can be seen in recent important legislation, such as India's National Rural Employment Government Scheme and the Right to Information Act. Key policymakers in the Government of India, very aware of China's different economic model, are under tremendous pressure from the Indian and foreign elites to invest resources in infrastructure development. But there is also an Indian context, informed by Gandhi's life and legacy, in which the number one priority should not be the infrastructure priority of the modern elites. Policymakers have to deal with grassroots social movements, articulated needs and demands and prospects of noncooperation and resistance. The result is that the Government of India has recently promoted the priorities of social programmes, 'inclusive growth' and 'inclusive democracy and development' over maximum infrastructure investment.

Third, something truly astounding occurred after the Mumbai terrorism of 2008, and this can only be fully understood by appreciating Gandhi's exemplary model and continuing influence. Considering the history of India–Pakistan wars and tensions, the ongoing Kashmir crisis, clear documentation of Pakistani-initiated and supported past terrorism and November 2008 terrorism within India, and Hindu–Muslim violent communal relations, one might have expected massive retaliation by India's military and by Indian Hindus. Indeed, after the 26–29 November terrorist attacks ended there were strong Hindu forces that, in both extreme rhetoric and calls for action, promoted using military force to finish Pakistan off once and for all and to repress 'unpatriotic' Indian Muslims.

Quite remarkably, often citing the philosophy and spirit of Mahatma Gandhi, India's Government and its Hindu and other masses showed tremendous self-restraint, resisted calls for violent retaliation, remained calm and rational in approaching the crisis and emphasized the need to preserve human rights and promote communal harmony. India's approach to this terrorism cannot be fully appreciated without taking into account the influence of Gandhi and his legacy. In the aftermath of Mumbai terrorism India demonstrates how an understandable concern with security and the need for justice can be integrated with a far greater intelligence, maturity, nonviolence and insistence on truth than was exhibited by 'modern' u.s. governmental, military and corporate interests after 9/11.

Fourth, Gandhi's legacy continues, often in unexpected ways, through his influence in popular culture and a continuing universal appeal. To provide but one of numerous possible illustrations, the 2006 Bollywood movie *Lage Raho Munnai Bhai*, directed by Rajkumar Hirani, became an unexpected huge hit in India, reviving interest in Gandhi, especially among a new generation. The movie has the Bollywood appeal of a musical comedy but what makes this film unusual is that the spirit of Mahatma Gandhi keeps appearing to the gangster don, Munnai Bhai. He gradually begins to promote what he calls 'Gandhigiri': how Gandhi principles can be put into practice in the everyday lives of ordinary people to help them solve their problems and to organize moral nonviolent protests. This movie led to a popular 'Gandhigiri' movement of how to apply Gandhi nonviolence and truth to one's life. It revived interest in Gandhi, especially among a younger generation, resulted in a sharp increase in sales of Gandhi books, established Gandhi as 'hip' and as a 'new pop icon' and has influenced millions to rethink their values and to consider the significance of Gandhi today.

The remarkable appeal of *Lage Raho Munnai Bhai*, not unlike the appeal of Attenborough's movie *Gandhi*, not only in India, but also to viewers throughout the world, raises the larger issue of Gandhi's continuing influence. On the one hand, on world leaders, such as u.s. President Barack Obama during his November 2010 visit to India, when he chose first to spend time at Mani Bhavan Gandhi Sangrahalaya in Mumbai. President Obama paid homage to Mahatma Gandhi, indicating that he looks to him for hope and inspiration and that Gandhi remains 'a hero not just to India but to the world'. On the other hand, on millions of ordinary students and citizens who, when exposed to Gandhi's writings and principles for the first time, experience Gandhi as touching something deep within them, as bringing out what we recognize as morally, culturally and spiritually best in us and desperately needed in the world.

Gandhi's greatest relevance today can be seen in his philosophy and approach to violence and nonviolence. Gandhi allows us to address our most pressing contemporary crises as expressions of our humanly caused, relational, economic, psychological, political, military, cultural, religious and other dimensions of violence and the dominant structural violence of the status quo. Gandhi provides ways for us to understand that perpetuating such multidimensional and structural violence will not lead to the resolution of contemporary crises of war, terrorism, civilizational disharmony and conflict, and environmental destruction. His philosophy also allows us to consider qualitatively different, transformative, preventative methods that offer some hope for a sustainable future of greater nonviolence, peace, truth, morality, love, compassion and meaningful ways of relating with integrity to all beings and to nature.

As has been shown, Gandhi's greatly broadened and deepened philosophy and approach to violence and nonviolence is integrally related ethically and ontologically to his philosophy and practice of truth. A selectively appropriated and creatively reformulated Gandhi-inspired approach provides a powerful critique of dominant characteristics of violent and untruthful modern civilization. It offers transformative nonviolent methods of noncooperation and resistance, along with the need to engage in constructive work to create alternative ethical and spiritual relations. Gandhi's philosophy of nonviolence offers desperately needed preventative approaches to violence and for conflict resolution, to deconditioning the dynamics of war-making and engaging in real peacebuilding, and to engaging in and transforming violent economic, religious and cultural conflicts. Gandhi's holistic, harmonious way of being in the world challenges us to consider unalienated and meaningful ways of relating to our self, to others and to nature; to live active, self-determining, meaningful, joyful lives of selfless service and integrity allowing for self-realization.

We may conclude our assessment of Gandhi today by considering two remarkable topics central to Gandhi's life and philosophy. Both topics have a profound relationship to crises in the twenty-first century. First, there is a key question regarding Gandhi's remarkable self, and, second, there is Gandhi's view of human evolutionary development and untapped human potential.

In chapter Six we observed how Gandhi equates self with truth, God and reality, and this is often used interchangeably with nonviolence and love. In this regard Gandhi repeatedly expresses his conviction that the entire purpose of life is self-realization, which is equivalent to truth-realization, God-realization and the realization of nonviolence and love. We observed that Gandhi uses 'self' in diverse ways, including the true individual inner self, the social relational self and the universal, unifying, absolute Self. We also noted that he often emphasizes the self as *swabhava*, one's unique, dynamic, individual, physical, mental and social self-nature to which each of us must be true in our relative, contextualized, relational path to greater self-realization.

The key question regarding Gandhi's self, that has inspired but also baffled even his admirers, is the following: what is the source of Gandhi's almost superhuman dedication, strength, fearlessness, and energy?[1] Even during the darkest periods of greatest personal despair, such as the time of unrestrained horror, terror and slaughter at Partition and his heroic pilgrimage through the devastated and hate-filled villages of Noakhali, where did Gandhi find the extraordinary strength and energy to struggle, suffer, sacrifice and serve as such an exemplary moral being?

In different contexts one can find diverse partial answers to this key question about Gandhi's self. Over the decades, through his many experiments with truth, Gandhi develops an extraordinarily strong will with a rare capacity to embrace sacrifice and voluntary suffering, to overcome his fears and act with courage, to take on vows and keep them and to undertake challenging commitments and fulfil them. This remarkable will allows Gandhi to embrace lofty ethical and spiritual ideals and then dedicate his life to making them a living reality. In many contexts of despair he also gains strength through his faith in God that Gandhi claims has always showed him the true way, or in truth and nonviolence that Gandhi claims have always emerged victorious throughout history.

The key to the source of Gandhi's dedication, strength, fearlessness and energy can best be identified with his philosophy and practice of renunciation. He finds the source for such self-development and self-realization in the Hindu tradition of the

Upanishads, Patanjali's *Yoga Sutra* and other religious and philosophical texts. For Gandhi the *Bhagavad-Gita* is his guide to daily living and is his best source for self-transformation and self-realization. He especially identifies with the *Gita*'s path of *karma yoga*, or renunciation in action, and with the last eighteen verses of Second Chapter, portraying the 'perfect sage' or ideal human being, upon which he meditated every day. He also asserts that this is a universal message that can be found in the Sermon on the Mount and in other lofty philosophical, ethical and spiritual texts throughout the world.

The key to the developed ethical and spiritual self is renunciation of ego-attachment to results with the performance of selfless service to meet the needs of others. Something remarkable occurs when one engages in the difficult transformative process of reducing one's ego to zero and engages in selfless service to meet the needs of others, especially the most disadvantaged.[2] This attitude and sense of purposive self is beautifully presented in Gandhi's famous 'A Talisman', remarkably written in August 1947, during Gandhi's last year and in the midst of overwhelming violence and terror.

> I will give you a talisman. Whenever you are in doubt, or when the self becomes too much with you, apply the following test. Recall the face of the poorest and the weakest man whom you may have seen and ask yourself if the step you contemplate is going to be of any use to him. Will he gain anything by it? Will it restore him to a control over his own life and destiny? In other words, will it lead to *swaraj* for the hungry and spiritually starving millions?
> Then you will find your doubts and yourself melting away.[3]

How does this renunciation of ego-attachment to results with the performance of selfless service lead to Gandhi's energy, endurance, fearlessness and strength? Gandhi asserts that when

Walking across a footbridge in Noakhali (East Bengal) during Gandhi's heroic mission to end the communal violence, November 1946.

we are motivated by ego-desires and attachments we worry about results, become entrapped in endless desires and needs, live fragmented lives without unified focus and lack self-rule and freedom. We experience daily lives of insecurity and multidimensional violence in which we construct violent defence mechanisms to protect the illusory ego. We live ego-defined lives of illusions and untruths that separate us from the unifying, interrelated, moral, spiritual and cosmic nature of reality.

Through his experiments with truth and gradual self-transformation Gandhi found that something remarkable occurs when one renounces such ego-attachments to results and engages in selfless service: one taps into incredible sources of energy, strength and creativity. Our ego-attached psychological, epistemological, moral and ontological obstacles and barriers arise from and perpetuate relations of fear, insecurity, violence and untruth. When they are removed, one is able to live a focused, integrated, empowered life of perseverance, fearlessness, peace, joy, and hope. By engaging in the process of reducing the ego-self to zero, embracing voluntary sacrifice (*yajna*) and suffering, and dedicating one's life to selfless service, Gandhi's transformative renunciation as self-realization allows him to harness incredible released energy. It allows him to live fully in the present as an integrated mind–body–heart whole, and to live an integrated life empowered by the laws and forces of love, nonviolence and truth.

It should be obvious that Gandhi's philosophy and practice of renunciation is diametrically opposed to the dominant modern economic, political, psychological, cultural, educational, consumerist orientations. We are repeatedly told that it is 'human nature' for human beings to be motivated by ego-desires and ego-attachments to results. That is the basis for working hard, personal growth, competitive success and creativity and innovation.

Support for Gandhi's alternative view of human motivation and the source of self-transformation and realization can be found in healthy, meaningful, personal, family and community living and also in great ethical and spiritual traditions throughout the world. Gandhi's alternative philosophy and practice of self and renunciation are especially relevant today because of the urgent growing conclusion that our present ego-defined desires, needs and attachments are extremely violent and economically and environmentally unsustainable. In addition there are some recent, rather startling, encouraging developments in the modern West that lend support for Gandhi's perspective. We shall mention only briefly two illustrations.

There are numerous self-help advocates with millions of devoted followers in the u.s., India and other parts of the world. Devotees are drawn overwhelmingly from the relatively privileged and usually successful sectors of the population. These 'modern' human beings experience ego-driven lives of great stress, alienation, meaninglessness and unfulfilment. Representative of such modern 'gurus' is Wayne Dyer, author of *The Power of Intention* and other best-selling works. Advocating a very positive and hopeful philosophy, Dyer is featured on television and at numerous other gatherings where enthusiastic participants embrace his message. Central to his message is the insightful observation that if we experience things negatively this creates a negative sense of our self and our world. In this regard the ego is an impediment. The ego separates us from the infinite, the creative source of all, of which we are a part and that is our true identity. Through our inner world of intentions, including surrounding ourselves with what is good, we connect to the invisible force, the infinite empowering source that allows us to awaken our 'divine' nature or true self. This is the key to our well-being and to living lives of meaning and happiness.[4]

What is revealing in Dyer's message, and what is representative of messages of numerous other modern 'gurus', is that it shares much with Gandhi's approach to the source of self-transformation and self-realization. In this regard it also critiques dominant characteristics of the modern ego-attached orientation as leading to illusion, stress, meaninglessness and alienation.

Of course, in appealing to a privileged Western audience and readership, the messages usually focus on the modern individual's personal well-being and happiness without including much of Gandhi's transformative philosophy and practice. Omitted is Gandhi's renunciation philosophy of the need for voluntary sacrifice, suffering, nonviolent struggle and resistance, and of how the privileged benefit from or are complicit with the structural violence and untruths of the status quo. Nevertheless, the widespread appeal of such modern approaches indicates some of the potential and relevance of a more comprehensive and more adequate Gandhi approach to our contemporary crises.

In addition there are numerous recent scientific studies that bring into question the effectiveness of modern ego-defined incentives in motivating human beings toward greater performance, even leaving aside questions of personal satisfaction, meaningful labour, morality, violence and truth. Best-selling author Daniel Pink reports on the latest 'science' on 'drive: the surprising truth about what motivates us'. He cites a study commissioned by the u.s. Federal Reserve Bank and conducted by top modern economists. They found that a system of higher monetary rewards, such as better payments and bonuses, along with punishments, does not produce better performance. In fact, in what would at first strike modern thinkers as 'counter-intuitive', they found that such ego-attached rewards had the opposite effect.[5]

It is true that when people are not paid enough, are living under necessity and are asked to perform the simplest straightforward tasks, ego-defined incentive rewards can motivate performance. This is the level at which Gandhi said that if people are suffering and living at the level of necessity, you first must address and fulfil their basic material needs. However, if people are paid enough to live comfortably and are engaged in more complex tasks, requiring some creative conceptual skill, the motivational structure of greater reward actually produces worse performance. According to Pink, what do numerous modern scientific studies tell us about what truly motivates us to better performance, leaving aside ethical, social, environmental and other concerns? There are three major factors that motive modern human beings to better performance: autonomy or self-direction (not unlike Gandhi's self-rule), mastery or the urge to get better, and purpose. In fact the science shows that when human beings have such a 'purpose motive' they perform better, are more creative and are often highly motivated to do skilled work in their extra time, without financial remuneration, and even to share or give away what they produce that is of value to others.

Once again these recent scientific studies may be seen as consistent with and lending credence to Gandhi's approach to the source of energy, motivation, creativity, meaning and perseverance of self-transformation and self-realization. Of course Gandhi goes far beyond these scientific motivational studies of raising performance level in economic productivity, athletics and other areas of human endeavour. Or, to put it differently, for Gandhi, 'performing better' includes developing character, renunciation and selfless service, voluntary sacrifice and self-realization based on truth and nonviolence. Nevertheless, one cannot overestimate the significance and relevance of modern scientific approaches that complement and may be integrated with a new Gandhi philosophy and practice for addressing contemporary crises.

Gandhi leaves us with a rather hopeful view of human potential and evolutionary development. Although Gandhi has an optimistic view of human beings as basically good, he rejects any absolute, rigid view of human nature. Gandhi is well aware of the incredible violence, untruths and humanly caused suffering throughout history. What he classifies as our 'brute' nature, our 'lower' nature, our 'animalistic' nature is part of our mode of being in the world. But human beings also experience and express our 'higher' mind–body–heart nature, our potential for developing love, nonviolence and truth that elevates and distinguishes us as truly human. For Gandhi there is unlimited potential for harnessing our ethical and spiritual capacities for self-transformation and realization.

Many modern thinkers reject Gandhi as a utopian dreamer who denies the dynamics of human evolutionary survival and development. Gandhi certainly rejects the kind of 'social Darwinism' with its version of 'survival of the fittest' defined by might makes right and whoever possesses the economic, political and military power is victorious. Gandhi, whose philosophy is much more compatible with Charles Darwin's approach to survival of the fittest in terms of natural selection and adaptability, claims that the brute force modern version is refuted by real human history and evolution. If humans behaved in such a brute manner, as is emphasized in history books and in the media, they would have become extinct long ago. What has allowed human beings to survive, evolve and flourish is our remarkable capacity for compassion and love; to be moved by the needs and suffering of others and to respond through selfless service. In other words, it is our 'higher' ethical and spiritual nature, our capacity to tap into love and nonviolent forces, soul and truth-forces, that provides the unifying force that allows us to realize our selves as integral parts of meaningful interconnected wholes. It is the self-realization of our higher nature that allows us to survive, develop and evolve.

What this means is that humankind today, faced with our severe crises, needs a radical, qualitatively different, paradigm shift as key to our evolutionary survival and development. We need new criteria for evaluating success, happiness, well-being, standard of living, development and progress. As Gandhi repeatedly asserts, we desperately need a more human-centric, moral-centric world view and way of being in the world. For Gandhi what is most significant and hopeful is that such a paradigm shift, away from the dominant modern violent civilizational orientation, is not an impractical romantic utopian dream. It is not an escape from reality. Indeed, it expresses tapping into and developing the ethical and spiritual forces and potential that are actualized every day in diverse ways.

Such a civilizational shift toward greater truth and nonviolence is not only humanly possible and relevant today, but it in reality defines what it is to live an unalienated, meaningful, creative, joyful, truly human existence.

References

Introduction

1 Tagore was probably not the first to confer this title on Gandhi. It is possible that the first to bestow the title 'Mahatma' on Gandhi was Nagar Sheth Nautamial B. Mehta on 21 January 1915 at Kamri Bai School, Jetpur, in Gujarat.

2 There is a common misconception regarding leading Indian politicians with the name 'Gandhi'. Jawaharlal Nehru (1889–1964), son of Congress Party leader Motilal Nehru (1861–1931), served as the first prime minister of independent India (1947–64). His daughter Indira (1917–1984) married Feroze Gandhi, who was not related to M. K. Gandhi. Indira Gandhi served as prime minister (1966–77, 1980–84). Her son Rajiv Gandhi (1944–1991) served as prime minister (1984–91). Rajiv's wife Sonia Gandhi is President of the Congress Party and is often described as the most powerful political figure in India. Their son Rahul Gandhi is one of India's rising political stars. These Gandhis represent a Nehru dynasty with no family relationship with Kasturba and Mohandas Gandhi.

3 The best resource for Gandhi's writing is the 100 volumes of M. K. Gandhi, *The Collected Works of Mahatma Gandhi* (CWMG; New Delhi, 1958–94). The CWMG was also released in a revised edition with interactive multimedia CD: M. K. Gandhi, *Mahatma Gandhi* (New Delhi, 1999). This led to a major controversy in which protestors charged that the revised edition with the CD-ROM was the result of incompetent editorial work, deletions and distortions of the original CWMG. The Government of India finally took the decision to withdraw the revised edition and CD-ROM.

4 In addition to the *Collected Works* and many publications with M. K. Gandhi as author, there are numerous excellent anthologies of Gandhi's writings. These include *The Moral and Political Writings of Mahatma Gandhi*, ed. Raghavan Iyer, 3 vols (Oxford, 1986–7); *The Mind of Mahatma Gandhi*, ed. R. K. Prabhu and U. R. Rao (Ahmedabad, 1967); and *The Oxford India Gandhi: Essential Writings*, ed. Gopalkrishna Gandhi (New Delhi, 2008).

5 There is a huge, diverse literature of writings on Gandhi's life and his thought. Major works that provide invaluable resources for biographical information include Gandhi's personal secretary Pyarelal (Pyarelal Nayar), *Mahatma Gandhi*, 5 vols plus 2 vols by his sister Sushila Nayar (Ahmedabad, 1956–94); biographer D. G. Tendulkar, *Mahatma: Life of Mohandas Karamchand Gandhi*, 8 vols (New Delhi, 1960); B. R. Nanda, *Mahatma Gandhi: A Biography* (New York, 1996); and Gandhi's grandson Rajmohan Gandhi, *Gandhi: The Man, His People, and the Empire* (Berkeley, CA, 2008). Briefer treatments of Gandhi's life and philosophy can be found in Bhikhu Parekh, *Gandhi: A Very Short Introduction* (Oxford, 2001) and *Gandhi's Experiments with Truth: Essential Writings by and about Mahatma Gandhi*, ed. Richard L. Johnson (Lanham, MD, 2006).

1 Youth in India and England

1 M. K. Gandhi, *An Autobiography: The Story of My Experiments with Truth* (Boston, 1993). Gandhi's *Autobiography* was first published in two volumes (Ahmedabad, 1927 and 1929).

2 In addition to Gandhi's *Autobiography*, Rajmohan Gandhi's *Gandhi: The Man, His People, and the Empire* (Berkeley, CA, 2008) provides a good description and analysis of Gandhi's youthful experiences.

3 Erik H Erikson, *Gandhi's Truth* (New York, 1969). There is a huge literature focusing on Gandhi's controversial attitudes toward sex and bodily desires. In chapter Five we consider the controversies around Gandhi's 'test', late in life, sleeping with his grandniece Manu and other naked young women.

2 South Africa

1 See M. K. Gandhi, *Satyagraha in South Africa*, trans. V. G. Desai (Ahmedabad, 1928) and M. K. Gandhi, *An Autobiography: The Story of My Experiments with Truth* (Boston, 1993).
2 Leo Tolstoy, *The Kingdom of God is Within You*, trans. A. Maude (Oxford, 1935) and 'Letter to a Hindoo', in *Mahatma Gandhi and Leo Tolstoy: Letters*, ed. B. S. Murthy (Long Beach, CA, 1987).
3 John Ruskin, *Unto This Last*, ed. P. M. Yarker (London, 1978).
4 'Gandhiji's Questions to Rajchandra and His Replies', in M. K. Gandhi, *The Collected Works of Mahatma Gandhi* (CWMG; New Delhi, 1969), XXXII, pp. 592–602.
5 M. K. Gandhi, *Hind Swaraj and Other Writings*, ed. Anthony J. Parel (Cambridge, 1997).

3 From the Return to India to the Salt March

1 Gandhi describes the major events in this chapter, from Champaran Satyagraha through Salt Satyagraha, in different volumes of M. K. Gandhi, *The Collected Works of Mahatma Gandhi* (CWMG). Many of these events appear in M. K. Gandhi, *An Autobiography: The Story of My Experiments with Truth* (Boston, 1993). There is also a huge literature by Gandhi's contemporaries and later scholars on all of these events. For example, for a description of the Champaran Satyagraha, see Judith M. Brown, *Gandhi: Prisoner of Hope* (Delhi, 1992), pp. 109–13.
2 Gandhi's later formulation of all of the following key parts of his Constructive Programme can be found in M. K. Gandhi, 'Constructive Programme: Its Meaning and Place', CWMG (New Delhi, 1979), LXXV, pp. 146–66.
3 Fred Dallmayr presents an overview of Gandhi's approach to Islam and Muslim leaders in 'Gandhi and Islam: A Heart-and-Mind Unity?' in his *Peace Talks – Who Will Listen?* (Notre Dame, IN, 2004). See Sheila McDonough, *Gandhi's Response to Islam* (New Delhi, 1994).
4 Gandhi describes the Salt Tax, Dandi March and Salt Satyagraha in many entries in CWMG (New Delhi, 1971), XLIII. The march and salt

civil disobedience, with the subsequent raid on the government salt depot in Dharasana, are dramatically portrayed in Attenborough's 1982 movie *Gandhi*.

4 From the Round Table to 'Constructive Work'

1 Romain Rolland, *Mahatma Gandhi* (London, 1924). The first biography of Gandhi had been written by South African minister Joseph J. Doke, *M. K. Gandhi* (Madras, 1909).

2 There is an extensive, diverse literature of writings by Gandhi, Ambedkar and others on the issues regarding untouchability and Ambedkar–Gandhi relations. See Thomas Pantham, 'Against Untouchability: The Discourses of Gandhi and Ambedkar', in *Humiliation*, ed. Gopal Guru (New Delhi, 2009), pp. 179–208, and Sudarshan Kapur, 'Gandhi, Ambedkar, and the Eradication of Untouchability', *Gandhi Marg*, xxxii/1 (2010), pp. 57–86.

3 M. K. Gandhi, 'Constructive Programme: Its Meaning and Place', *The Collected Works of Mahatma Gandhi* (*CWMG*; New Delhi, 1979), LXXV, pp. 146–66 (dated 13 December 1941).

4 Gandhi's critique of 'modern' economics and his alternative approach to economics are developed in chapters Seven and Eight. Gandhi's views on modern economics, capitalism and socialism are sometimes uncritical and confused and at other times insightful and extremely relevant today. I review Gandhi's writings on economics and interpret his strengths and weaknesses in Douglas Allen, 'Gandhi and Socialism', *International Journal of Gandhi Studies*, I (2011), pp. 107–35.

5 There is an extensive literature by and about Gandhi focusing on his approach to education. See M. P. Mattai, *Mahatma Gandhi's World-view* (New Delhi, 2000), especially 'Educational Order' (pp. 214–25), and 'On Education' in *Selections from Gandhi*, ed. Nirmal Kumar Bose (Ahmedabad, 1996), pp. 281–98. I provide extensive documentation from Gandhi's writings, as well as analysis of his controversial and insightful philosophy of education, in Douglas Allen, 'Mahatma Gandhi's Philosophy of Violence, Nonviolence, and Education', in *The Philosophy of Mahatma Gandhi for the Twenty-First Century*, ed. Douglas Allen (Lanham, MD, 2008 and New Delhi, 2009).

6 Chandalal Bhagubhai Dalal, *Harilal Gandhi: A Life* (Delhi, 2007) and the movie *Gandhi, My Father* (2007), based on Dalal's book, present a very different M. K. Gandhi as seen largely through the point of view and tragic life of his son.

7 See M. K. Gandhi, CWMG, xxviii (New Delhi, 1968), p. 365 (first published in *Young India*, 22 October 1925). The Seven Social Sins are formulated as Politics without principles, Wealth without work, Pleasure without conscience, Knowledge without character, Commerce without morality, Science without humanity and Worship without sacrifice. Although these seven social sins are embraced by Gandhi in his philosophy and practices, as expressed through his constructive work, he indicates in this writing that the specific formulation was sent to him by an unnamed 'fair friend'.

5 From 'Quit India' to Gandhi's Assassination

1 See Margaret Chatterjee, *Gandhi and His Jewish Friends* (Basingstoke, 1992).

2 For Gandhi's advice to Jews in Germany in November 1938 and his response to critics, see M. K. Gandhi, *The Collected Works of Mahatma Gandhi* (CWMG; New Delhi, 1977), LXVIII, pp. 137–41, 189–91, 191–3, 202–3, 276–8 and 382. For Buber's response to Gandhi, see Martin Buber and Judah Magnes, *Two Letters to Gandhi* (Jerusalem, 1939). See also Dennis Dalton, *Mahatma Gandhi: Nonviolent Power in Action* (New York, 1993), pp. 134–8 and 228.

3 M. K. Gandhi, CWMG (New Delhi, 1977), LXX, pp. 20–21. Gandhi indicates that friends urged him to send his brief, very polite plea to Hitler. The Raj Government did not permit the letter to be delivered.

4 In chapter Six, using the controversial illustrations of Hitler and Nazi power and the 26/11 Mumbai and other terrorism that are often used to dismiss Gandhi's approach, I shall present interpretations and extended analysis submitting that Gandhi's philosophy and approach, reformulated in new creative ways, are very insightful and relevant when responding to these most difficult anti-Gandhi illustrations.

5 The controversial topic of Gandhi sleeping with naked young women late in his life has received a lot of attention in popular and scholarly

writings in recent years. Gandhi is very open in discussions and writings about his controversial *brahmacharya* experiments. See, for example, M. K. Gandhi, *CWMG* (New Delhi, 1983), LXXXVII, p. 108. The best-known case of a young woman sleeping naked with Gandhi is that of his grandniece, Manu Gandhi, who later wrote the book *Bapu, My Mother* (Ahmedabad, 1949). Rajmohan Gandhi gives an account of Gandhi's *brahmacharya* tests with Manu in *Gandhi: The Man, His People, and the Empire* (Berkeley, CA, 2008), pp. 492–3 and 548–55. Nicholas Gier analyses many of these controversial issues in 'Was Gandhi a Tantric?' *Gandhi Marg*, XXIX/1 (2007), pp. 21–36.

6 Nirmal Kumar Bose, *My Days with Gandhi* (New Delhi, 1974). Another account by one of Gandhi's closest associates can be found in Pyarelal, *Mahatma Gandhi: The Last Phase*, I (Ahmedabad, 1956). As compiled in M. K. Gandhi, *CWMG*, there are many responses by Gandhi to his critics.

7 *The Statesman* (Calcutta, 6 September 1947), as cited by Rajmohan Gandhi, *Gandhi*, p. 615.

8 Cited by Dalton, *Mahatma Gandhi*, pp. 158–9.

9 This payment to Pakistan is Gandhi's final 'crime' against India and Hinduism, according to Gandhi's assassin Nathuran Godse and many militant Hindu nationalists even today. Gandhi's approval of the Indian Army's use of violent force in Kashmir to stop Pakistani-supported aggression also continues to be the source of some debate and controversy.

6 Gandhi's Philosophy: Truth and Nonviolence

1 Most of the analysis of Gandhi's philosophy of truth and nonviolence in this chapter is based on my previous writings, including the following: 'Gandhi, Contemporary Political Thinking, and Self-Other Relations', in *Gandhi's Experiments with Truth*, ed. Richard L. Johnson (Lanham, MD, 2005), pp. 303–29; 'Mahatma Gandhi's Philosophy of Violence, Nonviolence, and Education', in *The Philosophy of Mahatma Gandhi for the Twenty-First Century*, ed. Douglas Allen (Lanham, MD, 2008; New Delhi, 2009), pp. 33–62; '*Hind Swaraj*: Hermeneutical Questions of Interpretation, Mythic Construction, and Contemporary

Relevance', *Journal of Contemporary Thought*, 30 (2009), pp. 5–32.

2 See Gandhi's one-page essay in *Contemporary Indian Philosophy*,
   ed. S. Radhakrishnan and J. H. Muirhead (London, 1936), p. 21,
   and M. K. Gandhi, *The Collected Works of Mahatma Gandhi* (*CWMG*;
   New Delhi, 1974), LX, pp. 106–7.

3 M. K. Gandhi, *Truth Is God* (Ahmedabad, 1990), p. 28 (first appeared
   in *Harijan*, 8 July 1933).

4 For example, while asserting that we have only relative truths and
   there is not one absolute standard of right, Gandhi claims that
   'terrorism must be held to be wrong in every case' and 'I do not
   regard killing or assassination or terrorism as good in any circum-
   stances whatsoever.' See Gandhi, 'Patriotism Run Mad', *CWMG*
   (New Delhi, 1967), XXV, p. 441–3, and 'My Friend, the Revolutionary',
   CWMG (New Delhi, 1967), XXVI, pp. 486–92.

5 Gandhi, *CWMG* (New Delhi, 1971), XXXVIII, pp. 404–5.

6 Gandhi, *CWMG* (New Delhi, 1970), XXXVII, pp. 348–49 (*Young India*,
   11 November 1928).

7 Allen, 'Gandhi, Contemporary Political Thinking', pp. 317–25.

8 Bhikhu Parekh, *Gandhi: A Very Short Introduction* (New York, 2001),
   pp. 56–9, 62, 94.

9 Gandhi, *CWMG* (New Delhi, 1968), XXX, p. 133 (*Young India*, 18 March
   1926). See Ronald J. Terchek, *Gandhi: Struggling for Autonomy*
   (Lanham, MD, 1998), pp. 111–12. Anthony J. Parel, in *Gandhi's
   Philosophy and the Quest for Harmony* (Cambridge, 2006), uses the
   framework of the Hindu 'four aims of life' to demonstrate how
   Gandhi does not devalue, but emphasizes, fulfilling the first aim of
   artha, our material, economic and political well-being in this world.

10 Gandhi, *CWMG* (New Delhi, 1981), LXXXIV, p. 229 (*Harijan*, 23 June
    1946), and M. K. Gandhi, *From Yeravda Mandir: Ashram Observances*,
    trans. V. G. Desai (Ahmedabad, 1933; 1957 edition), pp. 12–13.

11 See, for example, Gandhi, *CWMG* (New Delhi, 1969), XXXII, pp. 401–2
    (*Young India*, 9 December 1926).

12 See chapter Five, notes 2 and 3.

13 M. K. Gandhi, *An Autobiography: The Story of My Experiments with
    Truth* (Boston, 1993), pp. xi–xii; Gandhi, *CWMG* (New Delhi, 1978),
    LXXI, p. 294 (*Harijan*, 2 March 1940); Gandhi, *CWMG* (New Delhi,
    1981), LXXXIV, p. 199 (*Harijan*, 2 June 1946).

14 Gandhi offers numerous formulations on the relations of cowardice, violence and nonviolence. See, for example, *CWMG* (New Delhi, 1965), XVIII, pp. 131–4 (*Young India*, 11 Aug. 1920); *CWMG* (New Delhi, 1967), XXIV, pp. 140–42 (*Young India*, 29 May 1926); *CWMG* (New Delhi, 1969), XXXI, p. 292 (*Young India*, 1 August 1926); *CWMG* (New Delhi, 1970), XLII, p. 73 (*Young India*, 10 Oct. 1929).

15 Gandhi, *CWMG* (New Delhi, 1969), XXXI, pp. 487–8 (*Young India*, 21 Oct. 1926).

16 Gandhi, *CWMG* (New Delhi, 1970), XXXVII, pp. 310–13 (*Young India*, 4 Oct. 1928); *CWMG* (New Delhi, 1981), LXXXIV, p. 62 (*Harijan*, 5 May 1946).

7 Modern Civilization, Religion and a New Paradigm

1 M. K. Gandhi, '1. Communal Unity', in 'Constructive Programme: Its Meaning and Place', *The Collected Works of Mahatma Gandhi* (*CWMG*; New Delhi, 1979), LXXV, pp. 147–9 (dated 13 December 1941).

2 M. K. Gandhi, *Hind Swaraj and Other Writings*, ed. Anthony J. Parel (Cambridge, 1997).

3 Gandhi, *Hind Swaraj*, pp. 6, 67, 106.

4 Ibid., pp. 68–70, 94–5.

5 Ibid., pp. 107–11.

6 Ibid., pp. 38, 43, 72, 103.

7 Ibid., p. 38.

8 Ibid., pp. 62–5.

9 One can find contrasting formulations in Gandhi's writings. In *Hind Swaraj*, p. 73, Gandhi follows his seemingly romantic, idyllic and utopian formulation of Indian villages by maintaining that such a *Swaraj* is not a dream but can be realized. In Gandhi's letter to Nehru of 5 October 1945, which appears in William L. Shirer, *Gandhi: A Memoir* (New York, 1979), pp. 36–8, he reasserts that he 'stands by his system of Government envisaged in *Hind Swaraj*' (written almost 36 years earlier). However, in this letter, reproduced in Parel's edition of *Hind Swaraj*, pp. 149–51, Gandhi presents a more flexible picture. He notes that he is not 'envisaging our village life as it is today' and that this is the 'village of my dreams still in my mind', but it is essential for

him to have a picture of this ideal village if he is to engage in the contemporary transformative process.

10 Gandhi's commentaries on the *Bhagavad-Gita* can be found in various pamphlets and in his *Collected Works*, especially CWMG (New Delhi, 1969), XXXII ('Discourses on the Gita'), pp. 94–376 and CWMG (New Delhi, 1970), XLI (*'Anasaktiyoga'*, published in English under the title *The Gita According to Gandhi*), pp. 90–133.

11 Gandhi, CWMG (New Delhi, 1969), XXXV, p. 492 (*Young India*, 19 January 1928): 'Hinduism with its message of ahimsa is to me the most glorious religion in the world – as my wife is to me the most beautiful woman in the world – but others may feel the same about their religion.' Gandhi, CWMG (New Delhi, 1970), XL, p. 58 (*Young India*, 21 March 1929): 'The most distinctive and the largest contribution of Hinduism to India's culture is the doctrine of ahimsa. It has given a definite bias to the history of the country for the last three thousand years and over and it has not ceased to be a living force in the lives of India's millions of even today. It is a growing doctrine, its message is still be delivered.'

12 See, for example, Lloyd I. Rudolph, 'Postmodern Gandhi', in *Postmodern Gandhi and Other Essays*, ed. Lloyd I. Rudolph and Susanne Hoeber Rudolph (Chicago, 2006), pp. 3–59. In *The Philosophy of Mahatma Gandhi for the Twenty-First Century*, ed. Douglas Allen (Lanham, MD, 2008; New Delhi, 2009), Nicholas F. Gier, 'Non-violence as Civic Virtue: Gandhi and Reformed Liberalism', pp. 121–42, and Naresh Dadhich, 'The Postmodern Discourse on Gandhi: Modernity and Truth', pp. 179–99, provide ways for interpreting Gandhi as 'postmodern'. In the same volume Makarand Paranjape, 'The "Sanatani" Mahatma: Rereading Gandhi Post-Hindutva', pp. 201–14, rejects the premodern–modern–postmodern classifications and submits that Gandhi should be interpreted as 'non-modern'.

13 Akeel Bilgrami, in 'Gandhi's Integrity: The Philosophy behind the Politics', in *Debating Gandhi*, ed. A. Raghuramaraju (New Delhi, 2006), pp. 248–66, and in other writings presents a very creative interpretation of Gandhi's radical critique of, and alternative to, dominant modern thinking.

14 Of the huge literature on Gandhi's approach to religion, special note may be made of Margaret Chatterjee, *Gandhi's Religious Thought* (London, 1983).

15 Gandhi, *Young India* (1 June 1921), p. 170. In the same passage Gandhi, while affirming his inclusive approach and openness to other cultural and religious influences, also emphasizes that 'I refuse to be blown off my feet by any. I refuse to live in other people's houses as an interloper, a beggar or a slave.'

16 For Gandhi's approach to religious scriptures, faith, and reason, see CWMG, XXI, p. 246; XXXI, pp. 24, 46; XXXIII, pp. 231–2; XLI, pp. 435–6, 468–9; LXIV, pp. 75, 397–402; LXXI, p. 294; LXXXIV, p. 199.

17 Bhikhu Parekh has excellent formulations on the Gandhi approach to religion, scriptures, reason, and his religious justification for tolerance, respect and interreligious dialogue. See, for example, chapter Three of Bhikhu Parekh, *Gandhi's Political Philosophy* (London, 1989) and Parekh, 'Gandhi and Interreligious Dialogue', in *The Philosophy of Mahatma Gandhi for the Twenty-First Century*, ed. Douglas Allen (Lanham, MD, 2008; New Delhi, 2009), pp. 1–17.

8 Gandhi Today

1 This is the major question raised by Eknath Easwaran in his *Gandhi the Man: The Story of His Transformation* (Tomales, CA, 1997).

2 See Gandhi, *The Collected Works of Mahatma Gandhi* (CWMG; New Delhi, 1969), XXXIII, p. 452 (written June 1927); Gandhi, *An Autobiography: The Story of My Experiments with Truth* (Boston, 1993), p. 420.

3 M. K. Gandhi, 'A Talisman', in D. G. Tendulkar, *Mahatma: Life of Mohandas Karamchand Gandhi*, VIII (New Delhi, 1960), p. 89.

4 Among Wayne Dyer's best-selling books, CDs, and DVDs are *The Power of Intention* (Carlsbad, CA, 2004) and *Excuses Begone!* (Carlsbad, CA, 2009).

5 Daniel H. Pink. *Drive: The Surprising Truth about What Motivates Us* (New York, 2009). See Daniel Pink's RSA (Royal Society for the Encouragement of the Arts, Manufactures and Commerce) Animate on YouTube with the same title.

Select Bibliography

Allen, Douglas, 'Gandhi and Socialism', *International Journal of Gandhi Studies*, 1 (2011), pp. 107–35
——, *'Hind Swaraj*: Hermeneutical Questions of Interpretation, Mythic Construction, and Contemporary Relevance', *Journal of Contemporary Thought*, 30 (2009), pp. 5–32
——, 'Mahatma Gandhi's Philosophy of Violence, Nonviolence, and Education', in *The Philosophy of Mahatma Gandhi for the Twenty-First Century*, ed. Douglas Allen (Lanham, MD, 2008 and New Delhi, 2009)
——, ed., *The Philosophy of Mahatma Gandhi for the Twenty-First Century* (Lanham, MD, 2008 and New Delhi, 2009)
——, 'Gandhi, Contemporary Political Thinking, and Self-Other Relations', in *Gandhi's Experiments with Truth*, ed. Richard L. Johnson (Lanham, MD, 2005)
Bilgrami, Akeel, 'Gandhi's Integrity: The Philosophy behind the Politics', in *Debating Gandhi*, ed. A. Raghuramaraju (New Delhi, 2006),
Bose, Nirmal Kumar, *My Days with Gandhi* (New Delhi, 1974)
Brown, Judith M., *Gandhi: Prisoner of Hope* (Delhi, 1992)
Buber, Martin and Judah Magnes, *Two Letters to Gandhi* (Jerusalem, 1939)
Chatterjee, Margaret, *Gandhi and His Jewish Friends* (Basingstoke, 1992)
——, *Gandhi's Religious Thought* (London, 1983)
Dadhich, Naresh, 'The Postmodern Discourse on Gandhi: Modernity and Truth', in *The Philosophy of Mahatma Gandhi for the Twenty-First Century*, ed. Douglas Allen (Lanham, MD, 2008; New Delhi, 2009)
Dalal, Chandalal Bhagubhai, *Harilal Gandhi: A Life* (Delhi, 2007)
Dallmayr, Fred, *Peace Talks – Who Will Listen?* (Notre Dame, IN, 2004)
Dalton, Dennis, *Mahatma Gandhi: Nonviolent Power in Action* (New York, 1993)

Desai, Mahadev, *The Gospel of Selfless Action or the Gita According to Gandhi* (Ahmedabad, 1946)

Doke, Joseph J., *M. K. Gandhi* (Madras, 1909)

Dyer, Wayne, *The Power of Intention* (Carlsbad, CA, 2004)

Easwaran, Eknath, *Gandhi the Man: The Story of his Transformation* (Tomales, CA, 1997)

Erikson, Erik H., *Gandhi's Truth* (New York, 1969)

Gandhi, Gopalkrishna, ed., *The Oxford India Gandhi: Essential Writings* (New Delhi, 2008)

Gandhi, M. K., *An Autobiography: The Story of My Experiments with Truth* (Boston, 1993)

——, *The Collected Works of Mahatma Gandhi*, 100 vols (New Delhi, 1958–94)

——, *From Yeravda Mandir: Ashram Observances*, trans. V. G. Desai (Ahmedabad, 1957)

——, *Hind Swaraj and Other Writings*, ed. Anthony J. Parel (Cambridge, 1997)

——, 'On Education' in *Selections from Gandhi*, ed. Nirmal Kumar Bose (Ahmedabad,1996)

——, *Satyagraha in South Africa*, trans. V. G. Desai (Ahmedabad, 1928)

——, 'A Talisman', in D. G. Tendulkar, *Mahatma: Life of Mohandas Karamchand Gandhi*, vol. VIII (New Delhi, 1960)

——, *Truth Is God* (Ahmedabad, 1990)

Gandhi, Manu, *Bapu, My Mother* (Ahmedabad, 1949)

Gandhi, Rajmohan, *Gandhi: The Man, his People, and the Empire* (Berkeley, CA, 2008)

Gier, Nicholas F., 'Nonviolence as Civic Virtue: Gandhi and Reformed Liberalism', in *The Philosophy of Mahatma Gandhi for the Twenty-First Century*, ed. Douglas Allen (Lanham, MD, 2008; New Delhi, 2009)

——, 'Was Gandhi a Tantric?' *Gandhi Marg*, XXIX/1 (2007), pp. 21–36

Iyer, Raghavan, ed., The *Moral and Political Writings of Mahatma Gandhi*, 3 vols (Oxford, 1986–7)

Johnson, Richard L., ed., *Gandhi's Experiments with Truth: Essential Writings by and about Mahatma Gandhi* (Lanham, MD, 2006)

Kapur, Sudarshan, 'Gandhi, Ambedkar, and the Eradication of Untouchability', *Gandhi Marg*, XXXII/1 (2010), pp. 57–86

Mattai, M. P., *Mahatma Gandhi's World-view* (New Delhi, 2000)

McDonough, Sheila, *Gandhi's Response to Islam* (New Delhi, 1994)

Nanda, B. R., *Mahatma Gandhi: A Biography* (New York, 1996)

Pantham, Thomas, 'Against Untouchability: The Discourses of Gandhi and Ambedkar', in *Humiliation*, ed. Gopal Guru (New Delhi, 2009)

Paranjape, Makarand, 'The "Sanatani" Mahatma: Rereading Gandhi Post-Hindutva', *The Philosophy of Mahatma Gandhi for the Twenty-First Century*, ed. Douglas Allen (Lanham, MD, 2008; New Delhi, 2009)

Parekh, Bhikhu, 'Gandhi and Interreligious Dialogue', in *The Philosophy of Mahatma Gandhi for the Twenty-First Century*, ed. Douglas Allen (Lanham, MD, 2008; New Delhi, 2009)

——, *Gandhi: A Very Short Introduction* (Oxford, 2001)

——, *Gandhi's Political Philosophy* (London, 1989)

Parel, Anthony J., *Gandhi's Philosophy and the Quest for Harmony* (Cambridge, 2006)

——, ed., *Hind Swaraj and Other Writings* (Cambridge, 1997)

Pink, Daniel H., *Drive: The Surprising Truth about What Motivates Us* (New York, 2009)

Prabhu, R. K. and U. R. Rao, eds, *The Mind of Mahatma Gandhi* (Ahmedabad, 1967)

Pyarelal (Pyarelal Nayar), *Mahatma Gandhi: The Early Phase* (Ahmedabad, 1965)

——, *Mahatma Gandhi: The Last Phase*, 2 vols (Ahmedabad, 1956)

Radhakrishnan, S. and J. H. Muirhead, eds, *Contemporary Indian Philosophy* (London, 1936)

Rolland, Romain, *Mahatma Gandhi* (London, 1924)

Rudolph, Lloyd I. and Susanne Hoeber Rudolph, eds, *Postmodern Gandhi and Other Essays* (Chicago, 2006)

Ruskin, John, *Unto This Last*, ed. P. M. Yarker (London, 1978)

Shirer, William L., *Gandhi: A Memoir* (New York, 1979)

Tendulkar, D. G., *Mahatma: Life of Mohandas Karamchand Gandhi*, 8 vols (New Delhi, 1960)

Terchek, Ronald J., *Gandhi: Struggling for Autonomy* (Lantham, MD, 1998)

Tolstoy, Leo, 'Letter to a Hindoo', in *Mahatma Gandhi and Leo Tolstoy: Letters*, ed. B. S. Murthy (Long Beach, CA, 1987)

——, *The Kingdom of God is Within You*, trans. A. Maude (Oxford, 1935)

Acknowledgements

I would especially like to acknowledge my appreciation to Ilze Petersons and Usha Thakkar for their kindness, feedback, and invaluable suggestions that helped me to research and write this book. Others, who engaged with me in beneficial discussions and provided me with helpful suggestions, and who often provided me with lecture and research opportunities, include, but are not limited to, the following: Bhikhu Parekh, Anthony Parel, Ashok Jhunjhunwala, Fred Dallmayr, Sandhya Mehta, Ramdas Bhatkal, Vasant Pradhan, Rajiv Vora, Niru Vora, Veena Howard, Prafulla Kar, Thomas Pantham, Naresh Kumar Sharma, Nagindas Sanghavi, Sushil Mittal, Joseph Prabhu, Nicholas Gier, Naresh Dadhich, Vinit Haksar, Richard Johnson, Makarand Paranjape, Arun Kumar, Michael Howard, Michael Barnhart, Karsten Struhl, Bal Ram Singh, G. Mishra, Priyankar Upadhhyaya, Hameed Khan, and Usha Gokani.

One of the many benefits of undertaking research on Mahatma Gandhi, as well as engaging in Gandhi-influenced practices, is that it brings you into meaningful relations with kind, ethical persons, who are remarkable for their selfless service in meeting the needs of others. I especially experienced such kindness from the dedicated staff at Mani Bhavan Gandhi Sangrahalaya in Mumbai, where I was based during my 2009–2010 sabbatical doing research for this book.

I appreciate the funding support for researching and writing this book that I received from the following sources: the Council for International Exchange of Scholars and the United States–India Educational Foundation for a Fulbright–Nehru Senior Research Fellowship for 2009–2010; the University of Maine Summer Faculty Research Award for Gandhi research during the summer of 2009.

Photo Acknowledgements

The author and publishers wish to express their thanks to the following sources of illustrative material and/or permission to reproduce it:

Photos © GandhiServe: pp. 6, 43, 102, 106, 109, 144; photo © Bob Fitch / GandhiServe: p. 11; photos © Vithalbhai Jhaveri / GandhiServe: pp. 9, 20, 21, 23, 29, 33, 37, 40, 42, 47, 51, 59, 63, 68, 71, 72, 73, 74, 85, 89, 92, 93, 156, 169; photo © Jagan Mehta / GandhiServe: p. 98.